PARABLES AND PARADOXES

FRANZ KAFKA

PARABLES AND PARADOXES

IN GERMAN AND ENGLISH

SCHOCKEN BOOKS / NEW YORK

First SCHOCKEN PAPERBACK edition 1961

Ninth Printing, 1974

Library of Congress Catalog Card No. 61-14917

Manufactured in the United States of America

CONTENTS

INHALT

PARABLES AND PARADOXES

Viele beklagen sich, dass die Worte der Weisen immer wieder nur Gleichnisse seien, aber unverwendbar im täglichen Leben, und nur dieses allein haben wir. Wenn der Weise sagt: "Gehe hinüber," so meint er nicht, dass man auf die andere Seite hinüber gehen solle, was man immerhin noch leisten könnte, wenn das Ergebnis des Weges wert wäre, sondern er meint irgendein sagenhaftes Drüben, etwas, das wir nicht kennen, das auch von ihm nicht näher zu bezeichnen ist und das uns also hier gar nichts helfen kann. Alle diese Gleichnisse wollen eigentlich nur sagen, dass das Unfassbare unfassbar ist, und das haben wir gewusst. Aber das, womit wir uns jeden Tag abmühen, sind andere Dinge.

Darauf sagte einer: "Warum wehrt ihr euch? Würdet ihr den Gleichnissen folgen, dann wäret ihr selbst Gleichnisse geworden und damit schon der täglichen Mühe frei."

Ein anderer sagte: "Ich wette, dass auch das ein Gleichnis ist."

Der erste sagte: "Du hast gewonnen."

Der zweite sagte: "Aber leider nur im Gleichnis."

Der erste sagte: "Nein, in Wirklichkeit; im Gleichnis hast du verloren."

Many complain that the words of the wise are always merely parables and of no use in daily life, which is the only life we have. When the sage says: "Go over," he does not mean that we should cross to some actual place, which we could do anyhow if the labor were worth it; he means some fabulous yonder, something unknown to us, something too that he cannot designate more precisely, and therefore cannot help us here in the very least. All these parables really set out to say merely that the incomprehensible is incomprehensible, and we know that already. But the cares we have to struggle with every day: that is a different matter.

Concerning this a man once said: Why such reluctance? If you only followed the parables you yourselves would become parables and with that rid of all your daily cares.

Another said: I bet that is also a parable.

The first said: You have won.

The second said: But unfortunately only in parable.

The first said: No, in reality: in parable you have lost.

Der Kaiser—so heisst es—hat dir, dem Einzelnen, dem
jämmerlichen Untertanen, dem winzig vor der kaiserlichen Sonne in die fernste Ferne geflüchteten Schatten, gerade dir hat der Kaiser von seinem Sterbebett
aus eine Botschaft gesendet. Den Boten hat er beim
Bett niederknien lassen und ihm die Botschaft ins Ohr
zugeflüstert; so sehr war ihm an ihr gelegen, dass er
sich sie noch ins Ohr wiedersagen liess. Durch Kopf-
nicken hat er die Richtigkeit des Gesagten bestätigt.
Und vor der ganzen Zuschauerschaft seines Todes—
alle hindernden Wände werden niedergebrochen und
auf den weit und hoch sich schwingenden Freitreppen
stehen im Ring die Grossen des Reichs—vor allen diesen hat er den Boten abgefertigt. Der Bote hat sich
gleich auf den Weg gemacht; ein kräftiger, ein uner-
müdlicher Mann; einmal diesen, einmal den andern
Arm vorstreckend, schafft er sich Bahn durch die
Menge; findet er Widerstand, zeigt er auf die Brust,
wo das Zeichen der Sonne ist; er kommt auch leicht
vorwärts, wie kein anderer. Aber die Menge ist so
gross; ihre Wohnstätten nehmen kein Ende. Öffnete
sich freies Feld, wie würde er fliegen, und bald wohl
hörtest du das herrliche Schlagen seiner Fäuste an
deiner Tür. Aber statt dessen, wie nutzlos müht er sich
ab; immer noch zwängt er sich durch die Gemächer
des innersten Palastes; niemals wird er sie überwinden;
und gelänge ihm dies, nichts wäre gewonnen; die Treppen hinab müsste er sich kämpfen; und gelänge ihm

The Emperor, so it runs, has sent a message to you, the humble subject, the insignificant shadow cowering in the remotest distance before the imperial sun; the Emperor from his deathbed has sent a message to you alone. He has commanded the messenger to kneel down by the bed, and has whispered the message to him; so much store did he lay on it that he ordered the messenger to whisper it back into his ear again. Then by a nod of the head he has confirmed that it is right. Yes, before the assembled spectators of his death—all the obstructing walls have been broken down, and on the spacious and loftily-mounting open staircases stand in a ring the great princes of the Empire—before all these he has delivered his message. The messenger immediately sets out on his journey; a powerful, an indefatigable man; now pushing with his right arm, now with his left, he cleaves a way for himself through the throng; if he encounters resistance he points to his breast, where the symbol of the sun glitters; the way, too, is made easier for him than it would be for any other man. But the multitudes are so vast; their numbers have no end. If he could reach the open fields how fast he would fly, and soon doubtless you would hear the welcome hammering of his fists on your door. But instead how vainly does he wear out his strength; still he is only making his way through the chambers of the innermost palace; never will he get to the end of them; and if he succeeded in that nothing would be gained;

dies, nichts wäre gewonnen; die Höfe wären zu durch-
messen; und nach den Höfen der zweite umschlies-
sende Palast; und wieder Treppen und Höfe; und
wieder ein Palast; und so weiter durch Jahrtausende;
und stürzte er endlich aus dem äussersten Tor—aber
niemals, niemals kann es geschehen—, liegt erst die
Residenzstadt vor ihm, die Mitte der Welt, hochge-
schüttet voll ihres Bodensatzes. Niemand dringt hier
durch und gar mit der Botschaft eines Toten.—Du aber
sitzest an deinem Fenster und erträumst sie dir, wenn
der Abend kommt.

he must fight his way next down the stair; and if he succeeded in that nothing would be gained; the courts would still have to be crossed; and after the courts the second outer palace; and once more stairs and courts; and once more another palace; and so on for thousands of years; and if at last he should burst through the outermost gate—but never, never can that happen—the imperial capital would lie before him, the center of the world, crammed to bursting with its own refuse. Nobody could fight his way through here, least of all one with a message from a dead man.—But you sit at your window when evening falls and dream it to yourself.

Wenn man aus solchen Erscheinungen folgern wollte, daß wir im Grunde gar keinen Kaiser haben, wäre man von der Wahrheit nicht weit entfernt. Immer wieder muß ich sagen: Es gibt vielleicht kein kaisertreueres Volk als das unsrige im Süden, aber die Treue kommt dem Kaiser nicht zugute. Zwar steht auf der kleinen Säule am Dorfausgang der heilige Drache und bläst huldigend seit Menschengedenken den feurigen Atem genau in die Richtung von Peking—aber Peking selbst ist den Leuten im Dorf viel fremder als das jenseitige Leben. Sollte es wirklich ein Dorf geben, wo Haus an Haus steht, Felder bedeckend, weiter als der Blick von unserem Hügel reicht und zwischen diesen Häusern stünden bei Tag und bei Nacht Menschen Kopf an Kopf? Leichter als eine solche Stadt sich vorzustellen ist es uns, zu glauben, Peking und sein Kaiser wäre eines, etwa eine Wolke, ruhig unter der Sonne sich wandelnd im Laufe der Zeiten.

Die Folge solcher Meinungen ist nun ein gewissermaßen freies, unbeherrschtes Leben. Keineswegs sittenlos, ich habe solche Sittenreinheit, wie in meiner Heimat, kaum jemals angetroffen auf meinen Reisen. —Aber doch ein Leben, das unter keinem gegenwärtigen Gesetze steht und nur der Weisung und Warnung gehorcht, die aus alten Zeiten zu uns herüberreicht. . . .

Eine Tugend ist diese Auffassung wohl nicht. Um

If from such appearances any one should draw the conclusion that in reality we have no Emperor, he would not be far from the truth. Over and over again it must be repeated: There is perhaps no people more faithful to the Emperor than ours in the south, but the Emperor derives no advantage from our fidelity. True, the sacred dragon stands on the little column at the end of our village, and ever since the beginning of human memory it has breathed out its fiery breath in the direction of Pekin in token of homage—but Pekin itself is far stranger to the people in our village than the next world. Can there really be a village where the houses stand side by side, covering all the fields for a greater distance than one can see from our hills, and can there be dense crowds of people packed between these houses day and night? We find it more difficult to picture such a city than to believe that Pekin and its Emperor are one, a cloud, say, peacefully voyaging beneath the sun in the course of the ages.

Now the result of holding such opinions is a life on the whole free and unconstrained. By no means immoral, however; hardly ever have I found in my travels such pure morals as in my native village. But yet a life that is subject to no contemporary law, and attends only to the exhortations and warnings which come to us from olden times. . . .

This attitude is certainly no virtue. All the more

so auffälliger ist es, daß gerade diese Schwäche eines
der wichtigsten Einigungsmittel unseres Volkes zu
sein scheint; ja, wenn man sich im Ausdruck soweit
vorwagen darf, geradezu der Boden, auf dem wir
leben. Hier einen Tadel ausführlich begründen, heißt
nicht an unserem Gewissen, sondern, was viel ärger
ist, an unseren Beinen rütteln.

remarkable is it that this very weakness should seem to be one of the greatest unifying influences among our people; indeed, if one may dare to use the expression, the very ground on which we live. To set about establishing a fundamental defect here would mean undermining not only our consciences, but, what is far worse, our feet.

EIN FRAGMENT

In diese Welt drang nun die Nachricht vom Mauer-
bau. Auch sie verspätet, etwa dreissig Jahre nach ihrer
Verkündigung. Es war an einem Sommerabend. Ich,
zehn Jahre alt, stand mit meinem Vater am Flussufer.
Gemäss der Bedeutung dieser oft besprochenen Stunde
erinnere ich mich der kleinsten Umstände. Er hielt
mich an der Hand, dies tat er mit Vorliebe bis in sein
hohes Alter, und mit der andern fuhr er seine lange,
ganz dünne Pfeife entlang, als wäre es eine Flöte. Sein
grosser, schütterer, starrer Bart ragte in die Luft, im
Genuss der Pfeife blickte er über den Fluss hinweg in
die Höhe. Desto tiefer senkte sich sein Zopf, der Gegenstand der Ehrfurcht der Kinder, leise rauschend auf
der golddurchwirkten Seide des Feiertagsgewandes.
Da hielt eine Barke vor uns, der Schiffer winkte
meinem Vater zu, er möge die Böschung herabkom-
men, er selbst stieg ihm entgegen. In der Mitte trafen
sie einander, der Schiffer flüsterte meinem Vater etwas
ins Ohr; um ihm ganz näherzukommen, umarmte er
ihn. Ich verstand die Reden nicht, sah nur, wie der
Vater die Nachricht nicht zu glauben schien, der Schiffer die Wahrheit zu bekräftigen suchte, der Vater noch
immer nicht glauben konnte, der Schiffer mit der Lei-
denschaftlichkeit des Schiffervolkes zum Beweis der
Wahrheit fast sein Kleid auf der Brust zerriss, der
Vater stiller wurde, und der Schiffer polternd in die

THE NEWS
OF THE BUILDING OF THE WALL

A FRAGMENT

The news of the building of the wall now penetrated into this world. This, too, arrived late, some thirty years after its announcement. It was on a summer's evening. Ten years old, I stood on the bank of the river with my father. As befits the significance of this much discussed moment, I remember the smallest circumstances. He held me by the hand—he liked to do that even when he was very old—and with his other hand he stroked his long and very thin pipe as if it were a flute. His large, sparse, stiff beard moved in the wind; enjoying his pipe, he looked upwards across the river. This made his pigtail, which was an object of reverence to children, sink lower, softly rustling against the gold-embroidered silk of his holiday gown. At that moment a bark came to a stop in front of us; the boatman beckoned to my father to descend the slope, while he himself climbed up to meet him. They met each other in the middle; the boatman whispered something into my father's ear. To get even closer to him, he embraced him. I did not understand what was said and saw only that my father did not seem to believe the news. The boatman tried to convince him that it was the truth, but Father still could not believe it; the boatman, with all the passion of a sailor, almost tore his clothes open on his breast in order to convince him that it was so. Father became

Barke sprang und wegfuhr. Nachdenklich wandte sich mein Vater zu mir, klopfte die Pfeife aus und steckte sie in den Gürtel, streichelte mir die Wange und zog meinen Kopf an sich. Das hatte ich am liebsten, es machte mich ganz fröhlich, und so kamen wir nach Hause. Dort dampfte schon der Reisbrei auf dem Tisch, einige Gäste waren versammelt, gerade wurde der Wein in die Becher geschüttet. Ohne darauf zu achten, begann mein Vater schon auf der Schwelle zu berichten, was er gehört hatte. Von den Worten habe ich natürlich keine genaue Erinnerung, der Sinn aber ging mir durch das Ausserordentliche der Umstände, von dem selbst das Kind bezwungen wurde, so tief ein, dass ich doch eine Art Wortlaut wiederzugeben mich getraue. Ich tue es deshalb, weil er für die Volksauffassung sehr bezeichnend war. Mein Vater sagte also etwa: Ein fremder Schiffer—ich kenne alle, die gewöhnlich hier vorüberfahren, dieser aber war fremd—hat mir eben erzählt, dass eine grosse Mauer gebaut werden soll, um den Kaiser zu schützen. Es versammeln sich nämlich oft vor dem kaiserlichen Palast die ungläubigen Völker, unter ihnen auch Dämonen, und schiessen ihre schwarzen Pfeile gegen den Kaiser.

quieter, and the boatman leaped back into the bark with a clatter and sailed away. Meditatively, my father turned back toward me, knocked out his pipe and stuck it in his belt, stroked my cheek, and pulled my head toward him. This was what I liked most, it made me very happy, and so we returned home. There the rice soup was already steaming on the table, several guests were already gathered, and the wine was just being poured into the cups. Without paying any attention to all this, my father began to report from the threshold what he had heard. Naturally, I have no exact recollection of his words, but because of the extraordinary nature of the circumstances involved, which was enough to impress even a child, their meaning sank into me so deeply that I still feel able to give a kind of verbatim version of them. And I do so now because these words were very characteristic of the popular interpretation. Thus, my father said more or less the following: A strange boatman—I know all those who usually sail past here, but this one was a stranger—has just told me that a great wall is going to be built to protect the Emperor. As you may know, the infidel nations, with demons among them too, often gather in front of the imperial palace and shoot their black arrows at the Emperor.

Zunächst muß man sich doch wohl sagen, daß damals
Leistungen vollbracht worden sind, die wenig hinter
dem Turmbau von Babel zurückstehen, an Gottge-
fälligkeit allerdings, wenigstens nach menschlicher
Rechnung, geradezu das Gegenteil jenes Baues darstel-
len. Ich erwähne dies, weil in den Anfangszeiten des
Baues ein Gelehrter ein Buch geschrieben hat, in
welchem er diese Vergleiche sehr genau zog. Er
suchte darin zu beweisen, daß der Turmbau zu Babel
keineswegs aus den allgemein behaupteten Ursachen
nicht zum Ziele geführt hat, oder daß wenigstens
unter diesen bekannten Ursachen sich nicht die aller-
ersten befinden. Seine Beweise bestanden nicht nur
aus Schriften und Berichten, sondern er wollte auch
am Orte selbst Untersuchungen angestellt und dabei
gefunden haben, daß der Bau an der Schwäche des
Fundamentes scheiterte und scheitern mußte. In dieser
Hinsicht allerdings war unsere Zeit jener längst ver-
gangenen weit überlegen. Fast jeder gebildete Zeit-
genosse war Maurer vom Fach und in der Frage
der Fundamentierung untrüglich. Dahin zielte aber
der Gelehrte gar nicht, sondern er behauptete, erst
die große Mauer werde zum erstenmal in der Men-
schenzeit ein sicheres Fundament für einen neuen
Babelturm schaffen. Also zuerst die Mauer und dann
der Turm. Das Buch war damals in aller Hände,
aber ich gestehe ein, daß ich noch heute nicht genau

THE GREAT WALL AND THE
TOWER OF BABEL

First, then, it must be said that in those days things
were achieved scarcely inferior to the construction of
the Tower of Babel, although as regards divine ap-
proval, at least according to human reckoning,
strongly at variance with that work. I say this because
during the early days of building a scholar wrote a
book in which he drew the comparison in the most
exhaustive way. In it he tried to prove that the Tower
of Babel failed to reach its goal, not because of the
reasons universally advanced, or at least that among
those recognised reasons the most important of all
was not to be found. His proofs were drawn not
merely from written documents and reports; he also
claimed to have made enquiries on the spot, and to
have discovered that the tower failed and was bound
to fail because of the weakness of the foundation. In
this respect at any rate our age was vastly superior
to that ancient one. Almost every educated man of our
time was a mason by profession and infallible in the
matter of laying foundations. That, however, was not
what our scholar was concerned to prove; for he
maintained that the Great Wall alone would provide for the first time in the history of mankind a
secure foundation for a new Tower of Babel. First
the wall, therefore, and then the tower. His book was
in everybody's hands at that time, but I admit that
even to-day I cannot quite make out how he conceived

begreife, wie er sich diesen Turmbau dachte. Die Mauer, die doch nicht einmal einen Kreis, sondern nur eine Art Viertel- oder Halbkreis bildete, sollte das Fundament eines Turmes abgeben? Das konnte doch nur in geistiger Hinsicht gemeint sein. Aber wozu dann die Mauer, die doch etwas Tatsächliches war, Ergebnis der Mühe und des Lebens von Hunderttausenden? Und wozu waren in dem Werk Pläne, allerdings nebelhafte Pläne, des Turmes gezeichnet und Vorschläge bis ins einzelne gemacht, wie man die Volkskraft in dem kräftigen neuen Werk zusammenfassen solle?

Es gab—dieses Buch ist nur ein Beispiel—viel Verwirrung der Köpfe damals, vielleicht gerade deshalb, weil sich so viele möglichst auf einen Zweck hin zu sammeln suchten. Das menschliche Wesen, leichtfertig in seinem Grund, von der Natur des auffliegenden Staubes, verträgt keine Fesselung; fesselt es sich selbst, wird es bald wahnsinnig an den Fesseln zu rütteln anfangen und Mauer, Kette und sich selbst in alle Himmelsrichtungen zerreißen.

this tower. How could the wall, which did not form even a circle, but only a sort of quarter or half-circle, provide the foundation for a tower? That could obviously be meant only in a spiritual sense. But in that case why build the actual wall, which after all was something concrete, the result of the lifelong labor of multitudes of people? And why were there in the book plans, somewhat nebulous plans, it must be admitted, of the tower, and proposals worked out in detail for mobilizing the people's energies for the stupendous new work?

There were many wild ideas in people's heads at that time—this scholar's book is only one example—perhaps simply because so many were trying to join forces as far as they could for the achievement of a single aim. Human nature, essentially changeable, unstable as the dust, can endure no restraint; if it binds itself it soon begins to tear madly at its bonds, until it rends everything asunder, the wall, the bonds and its very self.

Die Vertreibung aus dem Paradies ist in ihrem Haupt-
teil ewig: Es ist also zwar die Vertreibung aus dem
Paradies endgültig, das Leben in der Welt unausweich-
lich, die Ewigkeit des Vorgangs aber (oder zeitlich
ausgedrückt: die ewige Wiederholung des Vorgangs)
macht es trotzdem möglich, dass wir nicht nur dauernd
im Paradiese bleiben konnten, sondern tatsächlich dort
dauernd sind, gleichgültig ob wir es hier wissen oder
nicht.

Warum klagen wir wegen des Sündenfalles? Nicht
seinetwegen sind wir aus dem Paradiese vertrieben
worden, sondern wegen des Baumes des Lebens, damit
wir nicht von ihm essen.

Wir sind nicht nur deshalb sündig, weil wir vom
Baum der Erkenntnis gegessen haben, sondern auch
deshalb, weil wir vom Baum des Lebens noch nicht gegessen haben. Sündig ist der Stand, in dem wir uns
befinden, unabhängig von Schuld.

Wir wurden geschaffen, um im Paradies zu leben,
das Paradies war bestimmt, uns zu dienen. Unsere
Bestimmung ist geändert worden; dass dies auch mit
der Bestimmung des Paradieses geschehen wäre, wird
nicht gesagt.

Wir wurden aus dem Paradies vertrieben, aber zer-

The expulsion from Paradise is in its main significance eternal: Consequently the expulsion from Paradise is final, and life in this world irrevocable, but the eternal nature of the occurrence (or, temporally expressed, the eternal recapitulation of the occurrence) makes it nevertheless possible that not only could we live continuously in Paradise, but that we are continuously there in actual fact, no matter whether we know it here or not.

Why do we lament over the fall of man? We were not driven out of Paradise because of it, but because of the Tree of Life, that we might not eat of it.

We are sinful not merely because we have eaten of the Tree of Knowledge, but also because we have not yet eaten of the Tree of Life. The state in which we find ourselves is sinful, quite independent of guilt.

We were fashioned to live in Paradise, and Paradise was destined to serve us. Our destiny has been altered; that this has also happened with the destiny of Paradise is not stated.

We were expelled from Paradise, but Paradise was not destroyed. In a sense our expulsion from Paradise was a stroke of luck, for had we not been expelled, Paradise would have had to be destroyed.

stört wurde es nicht. Die Vertreibung aus dem Paradies war in einem Sinne ein Glück, denn wären wir nicht vertrieben worden, hätte das Paradies zerstört werden müssen.

Gott sagte, dass Adam am Tage, da er vom Baume der Erkenntnis essen werde, sterben müsse. Nach Gott sollte die augenblickliche Folge des Essens vom Baume der Erkenntnis der Tod sein, nach der Schlange (wenigstens konnte man sie dahin verstehen) die göttliche Gleichwerdung. Beides war in ähnlicher Weise unrichtig. Die Menschen starben nicht, sondern wurden sterblich, sie wurden nicht Gott gleich, aber erhielten eine unentbehrliche Fähigkeit, es zu werden. Beides war auch in ähnlicher Weise richtig. Nicht der Mensch starb, aber der paradiesische Mensch, sie wurden nicht Gott, aber das göttliche Erkennen.

Er ist ein freier und gesicherter Bürger der Erde, denn er ist an eine Kette gelegt, die lang genug ist, um ihm alle irdischen Räume frei zu geben, und doch nur so lang, dass nichts ihn über die Grenzen der Erde reissen kann. Gleichzeitig aber ist er auch ein freier und gesicherter Bürger des Himmels, denn er ist auch an eine ähnlich berechnete Himmelskette gelegt. Will er nun auf die Erde, drosselt ihn das Halsband des Himmels, will er in den Himmel, jenes der Erde. Und trotzdem hat er alle Möglichkeiten und fühlt es; ja, er weigert sich sogar, das Ganze auf einen Fehler bei der ersten Fesselung zurückzuführen.

God said that Adam would have to die on the day he ate of the Tree of Knowledge. According to God, the instantaneous result of eating of the Tree of Knowledge would be death; according to the serpent (at least it can be understood so), it would be equality with God. Both were wrong in similar ways. Men did not die, but became mortal; they did not become like God, but received the indispensable capacity to become so. Both were right in similar ways. Man did not die, but the paradisiacal man did; men did not become God, but divine knowledge.

He is a free and secure citizen of the world, for he is fettered to a chain which is long enough to give him the freedom of all earthly space, and yet only so long that nothing can drag him past the frontiers of the world. But simultaneously he is a free and secure citizen of Heaven as well, for he is also fettered by a similarly designed heavenly chain. So that if he heads, say, for the earth, his heavenly collar throttles him, and if he heads for Heaven, his earthly one does the same. And yet all the possibilities are his, and he feels it; more, he actually refuses to account for the deadlock by an error in the original fettering.

Since the Fall we have been essentially equal in our capacity to recognize good and evil; nonetheless it is just here that we seek to show our individual superiority. But the real differences begin beyond that knowledge. The opposite illusion may be explained thus: nobody can remain content with the mere knowl-

Seit dem Sündenfall sind wir in der Fähigkeit zur Erkenntnis des Guten und Bösen im Wesentlichen gleich; trotzdem suchen wir gerade hier unsere besonderen Vorzüge. Aber erst jenseits dieser Erkenntnis beginnen die wahren Verschiedenheiten. Der gegenteilige Schein wird durch folgendes hervorgerufen: Niemand kann sich mit der Erkenntnis allein begnügen, sondern muss sich bestreben, ihr gemäss zu handeln. Dazu aber ist ihm die Kraft nicht mitgegeben, er muss daher sich zerstören, selbst auf die Gefahr hin, sogar dadurch die notwendige Kraft nicht zu erhalten, aber es bleibt ihm nichts anderes übrig als dieser letzte Versuch. (Das ist auch der Sinn der Todesdrohung beim Verbot des Essens vom Baume der Erkenntnis; vielleicht ist das auch der ursprüngliche Sinn des natürlichen Todes.) Vor diesem Versuch nun fürchtet er sich; lieber will er die Erkenntnis des Guten und Bösen rückgängig machen, (die Bezeichnung: "Sündenfall" geht auf diese Angst zurück); aber das Geschehene kann nicht rückgängig gemacht, sondern nur getrübt werden. Zu diesem Zweck entstehen die Motivationen. Die ganze Welt ist ihrer voll, ja die ganze sichtbare Welt ist vielleicht nichts anderes als eine Motivation des einen Augenblick lang ruhenwollenden Menschen. Ein Versuch, die Tatsache der Erkenntnis zu fälschen, die Erkenntnis erst zum Ziel zu machen.

edge of good and evil in itself, but must endeavor as well to act in accordance with it. The strength to do so, however, is not likewise given him, consequently he must destroy himself trying to do so, at the risk of not achieving the necessary strength even then; yet there remains nothing for him but this final attempt. (That is moreover the meaning of the threat of death attached to eating of the Tree of Knowledge; perhaps too it was the original meaning of natural death.) Now, faced with this attempt, man is filled with fear; he prefers to annul his knowledge of good and evil (the term, "the fall of man," may be traced back to that fear); yet the accomplished cannot be annulled, but only confused. It was for this purpose that our rationalizations were created. The whole world is full of them, indeed the whole visible world is perhaps nothing more than the rationalization of a man who wants to find peace for a moment. An attempt to falsify the actuality of knowledge, to regard knowledge as a goal still to be reached.

DER TURM ZU BABEL

Wenn es möglich gewesen wäre, den Turm von Babel zu erbauen ohne ihn zu erklettern, es wäre erlaubt worden.

DER SCHACHT VON BABEL

Was baust du?—Ich will einen Gang graben. Es muß ein Fortschritt geschehn. Zu hoch oben ist mein Standort.

Wir graben den Schacht von Babel.

THE TOWER OF BABEL

If it had been possible to build the Tower of Babel without ascending it, the work would have been permitted.

THE PIT OF BABEL

What are you building?—I want to dig a subterranean passage. Some progress must be made. My station up there is much too high.

We are digging the pit of Babel.

Anfangs war beim babylonischen Turmbau alles in
leidlicher Ordnung; ja, die Ordnung war vielleicht zu
gross, man dachte zu sehr an Wegweiser, Dolmetscher,
Arbeiterunterkünfte und Verbindungswege, so als
habe man Jahrhunderte freier Arbeitsmöglichkeit vor
sich. Die damals herrschende Meinung ging sogar dahin, man könne gar nicht langsam genug bauen; man
musste diese Meinung gar nicht sehr übertreiben und
konnte überhaupt davor zurückschrecken, die Funda-
mente zu legen. Man argumentierte nämlich so: Das
Wesentliche des ganzen Unternehmens ist der Gedanke, einen bis in den Himmel reichenden Turm zu
bauen. Neben diesem Gedanken ist alles andere ne-
bensächlich. Der Gedanke, einmal in seiner Grösse
gefasst, kann nicht mehr verschwinden; solange es
Menschen gibt, wird auch der starke Wunsch da sein,
den Turm zu Ende zu bauen. In dieser Hinsicht aber
muss man wegen der Zukunft keine Sorgen haben, im
Gegenteil, das Wissen der Menschheit steigert sich, die
Baukunst hat Fortschritte gemacht und wird weitere
Fortschritte machen, eine Arbeit, zu der wir ein Jahr
brauchen, wird in hundert Jahren vielleicht in einem
halben Jahr geleistet werden und überdies besser, halt-
barer. Warum also schon heute sich an die Grenze der
Kräfte abmühen? Das hätte nur dann Sinn, wenn man
hoffen könnte, den Turm in der Zeit einer Generation
aufzubauen. Das aber war auf keine Weise zu erwarten. Eher liess sich denken, dass die nächste Generation

At first all the arrangements for building the Tower of Babel were characterized by fairly good order; indeed the order was perhaps too perfect, too much thought was taken for guides, interpreters, accommodation for the workmen, and roads of communication, as if there were centuries before one to do the work in. In fact the general opinion at that time was that one simply could not build too slowly; a very little insistence on this would have sufficed to make one hesitate to lay the foundations at all. People argued in this way: The essential thing in the whole business is the idea of building a tower that will reach to heaven. In comparison with that idea everything else is secondary. The idea, once seized in its magnitude, can never vanish again; so long as there are men on the earth there will be also the irresistible desire to complete the building. That being so, however, one need have no anxiety about the future; on the contrary, human knowledge is increasing, the art of building has made progress and will make further progress, a piece of work which takes us a year may perhaps be done in half the time in another hundred years, and better done, too, more enduringly. So why exert oneself to the extreme limit of one's present powers? There would be some sense in doing that only if it were likely that the tower could be completed in one generation. But that is beyond all hope. It is far more likely that the next generation with their perfected knowledge will find the work of their

mit ihrem vervollkommneten Wissen die Arbeit der vorigen Generation schlecht finden und das Gebaute niederreissen werde, um von neuem anzufangen. Solche Gedanken lähmten die Kräfte, und mehr als um den Turmbau kümmerte man sich um den Bau der Arbeiterstadt. Jede Landsmannschaft wollte das schönste Quartier haben, dadurch ergaben sich Streitigkeiten, die sich bis zu blutigen Kämpfen steigerten. Diese Kämpfe hörten nicht mehr auf; den Führern waren sie ein neues Argument dafür, dass der Turm auch mangels der nötigen Konzentration sehr langsam oder lieber erst nach allgemeinem Friedensschluss gebaut werden sollte. Doch verbrachte man die Zeit nicht nur mit Kämpfen, in den Pausen verschönerte man die Stadt, wodurch man allerdings neuen Neid und neue Kämpfe hervorrief. So verging die Zeit der ersten Generation, aber keine der folgenden war anders, nur die Kunstfertigkeit steigerte sich immerfort und damit die Kampfsucht. Dazu kam, dass schon die zweite oder dritte Generation die Sinnlosigkeit des Himmelsturmbaus erkannte, doch war man schon viel zu sehr miteinander verbunden, um die Stadt zu verlassen.

Alles was in dieser Stadt an Sagen und Liedern entstanden ist, ist erfüllt von der Sehnsucht nach einem prophezeiten Tag, an welchem die Stadt von einer Riesenfaust in fünf kurz aufeinanderfolgenden Schlägen zerschmettert werden wird. Deshalb hat auch die Stadt die Faust im Wappen.

predecessors bad, and tear down what has been built so as to begin anew. Such thoughts paralyzed people's powers, and so they troubled less about the tower than the construction of a city for the workmen. Every nationality wanted the finest quarters for itself, and this gave rise to disputes, which developed into bloody conflicts. These conflicts never came to an end; to the leaders they were a new proof that, in the absence of the necessary unity, the building of the tower must be done very slowly, or indeed preferably postponed until universal peace was declared. But the time was spent not only in conflict; the town was embellished in the intervals, and this unfortunately enough evoked fresh envy and fresh conflict. In this fashion the age of the first generation went past, but none of the succeeding ones showed any difference; except that technical skill increased and with it occasion for conflict. To this must be added that the second or third generation had already recognized the senselessness of building a heaven-reaching tower; but by that time everybody was too deeply involved to leave the city.

All the legends and songs that came to birth in that city are filled with longing for a prophesied day when the city would be destroyed by five successive blows from a gigantic fist. It is for that reason too that the city has a closed fist on its coat of arms.

Abrahams geistige Armut und die Schwerbeweglichkeit dieser Armut ist ein Vorteil, sie erleichtert ihm die Konzentration oder vielmehr sie ist schon Konzentration, wodurch er allerdings den Vorteil verliert, der in der Anwendung der Konzentrationskraft liegt.

Abraham ist in folgender Täuschung begriffen: Die Einförmigkeit dieser Welt kann er nicht ertragen. Nun ist aber die Welt bekanntlich ungemein mannigfaltig, was jederzeit nachzuprüfen ist, indem man eine Handvoll Welt nimmt und näher ansieht. Die Klage über die Einförmigkeit der Welt ist also eigentlich eine Klage über nicht genügend tiefe Vermischung mit der Mannigfaltigkeit der Welt.

Ich könnte mir einen anderen Abraham denken,— der freilich würde es nicht bis zum Erzvater bringen, nicht einmal bis zum Altkeiderhändler—der die Forderung des Opfers sofort, bereitwillig wie ein Kellner, zu erfüllen bereit wäre, der das Opfer aber doch nicht zustande brächte, weil er von zuhause nicht fort kann, er ist unentbehrlich, die Wirtschaft benötigt ihn, immerfort ist noch etwas anzuordnen, das Haus ist nicht fertig, aber ohne dass sein Haus fertig ist, ohne diesen Rückhalt kann er nicht fort, das sieht auch die Bibel ein, denn sie sagt: "er bestellte sein Haus," und Abraham hatte wirklich alles in Fülle schon vorher; wenn

Abraham's spiritual poverty and the inertia of this poverty are an asset, they make concentration easier for him, or, even more, they are concentration already —by this, however, he loses the advantage that lies in applying the powers of concentration.

Abraham falls victim to the following illusion: he cannot stand the uniformity of this world. Now the world is known, however, to be uncommonly various, which can be verified at any time by taking a handful of world and looking at it closely. Thus this complaint at the uniformity of the world is really a complaint at not having been mixed profoundly enough with the diversity of the world.

I could conceive of another Abraham for myself— he certainly would have never gotten to be a patriarch or even an old-clothes dealer—who was prepared to satisfy the demand for a sacrifice immediately, with the promptness of a waiter, but was unable to bring it off because he could not get away, being indispensable; the household needed him, there was perpetually something or other to put in order, the house was never ready; for without having his house ready, without having something to fall back on, he could not leave —this the Bible also realized, for it says: "He set his house in order." And, in fact, Abraham possessed

er nicht das Haus gehabt hätte, wo hätte er denn sonst den Sohn aufgezogen, in welchem Balken das Opfermesser stecken gehabt?

Dieser Abraham—aber es sind alte Geschichten, nicht mehr der Rede wert. Besonders der wirkliche Abraham nicht, er hat schon vorher alles gehabt, wurde von der Kindheit an dazu geführt, ich kann den Sprung nicht sehen. Wenn er schon alles hatte und doch noch höher geführt werden sollte, musste ihm nun, wenigstens scheinbar, etwas fortgenommen werden, das ist folgerichtig und kein Sprung. Anders die anderen Abrahame, die stehen auf ihrem Bauplatz und sollen nun plötzlich auf den Berg Morija; womöglich haben sie noch nicht einmal einen Sohn und sollen ihn schon opfern. Das sind Unmöglichkeiten und Sarah hat recht, wenn sie lacht. Bleibt also nur der Verdacht, dass diese Männer absichtlich mit ihrem Haus nicht fertig werden und—um ein sehr grosses Beispiel zu nennen—das Gesicht in magischen Trilogien verstekken, um es nicht heben zu müssen und den Berg zu sehen, der in der Ferne steht.

Aber ein anderer Abraham. Einer der durchaus richtig opfern will und überhaupt die richtige Witterung für die ganze Sache hat, aber nicht glauben kann, dass er gemeint ist, er, der widerliche alte Mann, und sein Kind, der schmutzige Junge. Ihm fehlt nicht der wahre Glaube, diesen Glauben hat er, er würde in der richtigen Verfassung opfern, wenn er nur glauben könnte, dass er gemeint ist. Er fürchtet, er werde zwar als Abraham mit dem Sohne ausreiten, aber auf dem Weg sich in Don Quichotte verwandeln. Über Abraham

everything in plenty to start with; if he had not had a house, where would he have raised his son, and in which rafter would he have stuck the sacrificial knife?

This Abraham—but it's all an old story not worth discussing any longer. Especially not the real Abraham; he had everything to start with, was brought up to it from childhood—I can't see the leap. If he already had everything, and yet was to be raised still higher, then something had to be taken away from him, at least in appearance: this would be logical and no leap. It was different for the other Abrahams, who stood in the houses they were building and suddenly had to go up on Mount Moriah; it is possible that they did not even have a son, yet already had to sacrifice him. These are impossibilities, and Sarah was right to laugh. Thus only the suspicion remains that it was by intention that these men did not ready their houses, and—to select a very great example—hid their faces in magic trilogies in order not to have to lift them and see the mountain standing in the distance.

But take another Abraham. One who wanted to perform the sacrifice altogether in the right way and had a correct sense in general of the whole affair, but could not believe that he was the one meant, he, an ugly old man, and the dirty youngster that was his child. True faith is not lacking to him, he has this faith; he would make the sacrifice in the right spirit if only he could believe he was the one meant. He is afraid that after starting out as Abraham with his son he would change on the way into Don Quixote. The world would have been enraged at Abraham could it have

wäre die Welt damals entsetzt gewesen, wenn sie zugesehen hätte, dieser aber fürchtet, die Welt werde sich bei dem Anblick totlachen. Es ist aber nicht die Lächerlichkeit an sich, die er fürchtet—allerdings fürchtet er auch sie, vor allem sein Mitlachen—hauptsächlich aber fürchtet er, dass diese Lächerlichkeit ihn noch älter und widerlicher, seinen Sohn noch schmutziger machen wird, noch unwürdiger, wirklich gerufen zu werden. Ein Abraham, der ungerufen kommt! Es ist so, wie wenn der beste Schüler feierlich am Schluss des Jahres eine Prämie bekommen soll und in der erwartungsvollen Stille der schlechteste Schüler infolge eines Hörfehlers aus seiner schmutzigen letzten Bank hervorkommt und die ganze Klasse losplatzt. Und es ist vielleicht gar kein Hörfehler, sein Name wurde wirklich genannt, die Belohnung des Besten soll nach Absicht des Lehrers gleichzeitig eine Bestrafung des Schlechtesten sein.

DER BERG SINAI

Viele umschleichen den Berg Sinai. Ihre Rede ist undeutlich, entweder sind sie redselig oder schreien sie oder sind sie verschlossen. Aber keiner von ihnen kommt geraden Wages herab auf einer breiten, neu entstandenen, glatten Straße, die ihrerseits die Schritte groß macht und beschleunigt.

beheld him at the time, but this one is afraid that the world would laugh itself to death at the sight of him. However, it is not the ridiculousness as such that he is afraid of—though he is, of course, afraid of that too and, above all, of his joining in the laughter—but in the main he is afraid that this ridiculousness will make him even older and uglier, his son even dirtier, even more unworthy of being really called. An Abraham who should come unsummoned! It is as if, at the end of the year, when the best student was solemnly about to receive a prize, the worst student rose in the expectant stillness and came forward from his dirty desk in the last row because he had made a mistake of hearing, and the whole class burst out laughing. And perhaps he had made no mistake at all, his name really was called, it having been the teacher's intention to make the rewarding of the best student at the same time a punishment for the worst one.

MOUNT SINAI

Many people prowl round Mount Sinai. Their speech is blurred, either they are garrulous or they shout or they are taciturn. But none of them comes straight down a broad, newly made, smooth road that does its own part in making one's strides long and swifter.

Alles fügte sich ihm zum Bau. Fremde Arbeiter brachten die Marmorsteine, zubehauen und zueinander gehörig. Nach den abmessenden Bewegungen seiner Finger hoben sich die Steine und verschoben sich. Kein Bau entstand jemals so leicht wie dieser Tempel oder vielmehr dieser Tempel entstand nach wahrer Tempelart. Nur dass auf jedem Stein—aus welchem Bruche stammten sie?—unbeholfenes Gekritzel sinnloser Kinderhände oder vielmehr Eintragungen barbarischer Gebirgsbewohner zum Ärger oder zur Schändung oder zu völliger Zerstörung mit offenbar grossartig scharfen Instrumenten für eine den Tempel überdauernde Ewigkeit eingeritzt waren.

Everything came to his aid during the construction work. Foreign workers brought the marble blocks, trimmed and fitted to one another. The stones rose and placed themselves according to the gauging motions of his fingers. No building ever came into being as easily as did this temple—or rather, this temple came into being the way a temple should. Except that, to wreak a spite or to desecrate or destroy it completely, instruments obviously of a magnificent sharpness had been used to scratch on every stone—from what quarry had they come?—for an eternity outlasting the temple, the clumsy scribblings of senseless children's hands, or rather the entries of barbaric mountain dwellers.

In unserer Synagoge lebt ein Tier in der Größe etwa eines Marders. Es ist oft sehr gut zu sehn, bis auf eine Entfernung von etwa zwei Metern duldet es das Herankommen der Menschen. Seine Farbe ist ein helles Blaugrün. Sein Fell hat noch niemand berührt, es läßt sich also darüber nichts sagen, fast möchte man behaupten, daß auch die wirkliche Farbe des Felles unbekannt ist, vielleicht stammt die sichtbare Farbe nur vom Staub und Mörtel, die sich im Fell verfangen haben, die Farbe ähnelt ja auch dem Verputz des Synagogeninnern, nur ist sie ein wenig heller. Es ist, von seiner Furchtsamkeit abgesehn, ein ungemein ruhiges seßhaftes Tier; würde es nicht so oft aufgescheucht werden, es würde wohl den Ort kaum wechseln, sein Lieblingsaufenthalt ist das Gitter der Frauenabteilung, mit sichtbarem Behagen krallt es sich in die Maschen des Gitters, streckt sich und blickt hinab in den Betraum, diese kühne Stellung scheint es zu freuen, aber der Tempeldiener hat den Auftrag, das Tier niemals am Gitter zu dulden, es würde sich an diesen Platz gewöhnen, und das kann man wegen der Frauen, die das Tier fürchten, nicht zulassen. Warum sie es fürchten, ist unklar. Es sieht allerdings beim ersten Anblick erschreckend aus, besonders der lange Hals, das dreikantige Gesicht, die fast waagrecht vorstehenden Oberzähne, über der Oberlippe eine Reihe langer, die Zähne überragender, offenbar ganz harter, heller

In our synagogue there lives an animal about the size of a marten. One can often get a very good view of it, for it allows people to approach to a distance of about six feet from it. It is pale blue-green in color. Nobody has ever yet touched its fur, and so nothing can be said about that, and one might almost go so far as to assert that the real color of its coat is unknown, perhaps the color one sees is only caused by the dust and mortar with which its fur is matted, and indeed the color does resemble that of the paint inside the synagogue, only it is a little brighter. Apart from its timidity, it is an uncommonly quiet animal of settled habits; if it were not so often disturbed, it would doubtless scarcely be in this place at all, its favorite haunt being the latticework in front of the women's compartment; with visible delight it sinks its claws into the lattice, stretching itself and gazing down into the main chamber; this audacious attitude seems to please it, but the beadle has instructions never to tolerate the animal's being on the lattice, for it would get used to the place, and that cannot be permitted on account of the women, who are afraid of the animal. Why they are afraid is not clear. True, at a first glance it looks frightening, particularly the long neck, the triangular face, the upper teeth, which jut out almost horizontally, and on the upper lip a row of long, obviously hard, pale bristles, which extend even farther than the teeth—all that may be frightening, but it does

49

Borstenhaare, das alles kann erschreken, aber bald muß man erkennen, wie ungefährlich dieser ganze scheinbare Schrecken ist. Vor allem hält es sich ja von den Menschen fern, es ist scheuer als ein Waldtier und scheint mit nichts als dem Gebäude verbunden und sein persönliches Unglück besteht wohl darin, daß dieses Gebäude eine Synagoge ist, also ein zeitweilig sehr belebter Ort. Könnte man sich mit dem Tier verständigen, könnte man es allerdings damit trösten, daß die Gemeinde unseres Bergstädtchens von Jahr zu Jahr kleiner wird und es ihr schon Mühe macht, die Kosten für die Erhaltung der Synagoge aufzubringen. Es ist nicht ausgeschlossen, daß in einiger Zeit aus der Synagoge ein Getreidespeicher wird oder dergleichen und daß das Tier die Ruhe bekommt, die ihm jetzt schmerzlich fehlt.

Es sind allerdings nur die Frauen, die das Tier fürchten, den Männern ist es längst gleichgültig geworden, eine Generation hat es der anderen gezeigt, immer wieder hat man es gesehn, schließlich hat man keinen Blick mehr daran gewendet und selbst die Kinder, die es zum erstenmal sehn, staunen nicht mehr. Es ist das Haustier der Synagoge geworden, warum sollte nicht die Synagoge ein besonders, nirgends sonst vorkommendes Haustier haben? Wären nicht die Frauen, man würde kaum mehr von der Existenz des Tieres wissen. Aber selbst die Frauen haben keine wirkliche Furcht vor dem Tier, es wäre auch zu sonderbar, ein solches Tier tagaus, tagein zu fürchten, jahre- und jahrzehntelang. Sie verteidigen sich zwar damit, daß ihnen das Tier meist viel näher ist als

not take one long to realize how harmless this whole apparent horror is. Above all, it keeps away from human beings, it is more shy than a denizen of the forest, and seems to be attached only to the building, and it is doubtless its personal misfortune that this building is a synagogue, that is, a place that is at times full of people. If only one could communicate with the animal, one could, of course, comfort it by telling it that the congregation in this little town of ours in the mountains is becoming smaller every year and that it is already having trouble in raising the money for the upkeep of the synagogue. It is not impossible that before long the synagogue will have become a granary or something of the sort and the animal will then have the peace it now so sorely lacks.

To be sure, it is only the women who are afraid of the animal, the men have long ceased to bother about it, one generation has pointed it out to the next, it has been seen over and over again, and by this time nobody any longer wastes a glance on it, until now even the children, seeing it for the first time, do not show any amazement. It has become that animal which belongs to the synagogue—why should not the synagogue have a special domestic animal not found anywhere else? If it were not for the women, one would hardly be aware of the animal's existence any more now at all. But even the women are not really afraid of the animal, indeed it would be more than odd to go on being afraid of such an animal, day in, day out, for years, for decades. Their excuse is that the animal is usually much nearer to them than to the

den Männern, und das ist richtig. Hinunter zu den Männern wagt sich das Tier nicht, niemals hat man es noch auf dem Fußboden gesehn. Läßt man es nicht zum Gitter der Frauenabteilung, so hält es sich wenigstens in gleicher Höhe auf der gegenüberliegenden Wand auf. Dort ist ein ganz schmaler Mauervorsprung, kaum zwei Finger breit, er umläuft drei Seiten der Synagoge, auf diesem Vorsprung huscht das Tier manchmal hin und her, meistens aber hockt es ruhig auf einer bestimmten Stelle gegenüber den Frauen. Es ist fast unbegreiflich, wie es diesen schmalen Weg so leicht benützen kann, und die Art, wie es dort oben, am Ende angekommen, wieder wendet, ist sehenswert, es ist doch schon ein sehr altes Tier, aber es zögert nicht, den gewagtesten Luftsprung zu machen, der auch niemals mißlingt, in der Luft hat es sich umgedreht und schon läuft es wieder seinen Weg zurück. Allerdings wenn man das einigemal gesehen hat, ist man gesättigt und hat keinen Anlaß, immerfort hinzustarren. Es ist ja auch weder Furcht noch Neugier, welche die Frauen in Bewegung hält, würden sie sich mehr mit dem Beten beschäftigen, könnten sie das Tier völlig vergessen, die frommen Frauen täten das auch, wenn es die andern, welche die große Mehrzahl sind, zuließen, diese aber wollen immer gern auf sich aufmerksam machen und das Tier ist ihnen dafür ein willkommener Vorwand. Wenn sie es könnten und wenn sie es wagten, hätten sie das Tier noch näher an sich gelockt, um noch mehr erschrecken zu dürfen. Aber in Wirklichkeit drängt sich ja das Tier gar nicht zu ihnen, es küm-

men, and this is true. The animal does not dare to go down below where the men are, it has never yet been seen on the floor. If it is stopped from getting on the lattice of the women's compartment, then at least it wants to be at the same height on the opposite wall. There, on a very narrow ledge scarcely two inches wide, which extends round three sides of the synagogue, the animal will sometimes flit to and fro, but mostly it sits quietly curled up on a certain spot opposite the women. It is almost incomprehensible how it so easily contrives to use this narrow path, and it is remarkable to see the way it turns round up there when it gets to the end, for after all, it is by now a very old animal, but it does not shrink from taking a most daring leap into the air, nor does it ever miss its foothold, and having turned in mid-air it runs straight back again the way it came. Of course, when one has seen this several times one has had enough of it, and there is no reason why one should go on staring. Nor is it either fear or curiosity that keeps the women fidgeting about; if they were to pay more attention to their prayers, they might be able to forget all about the animal; the devout women would certainly do so if the others, who are in the great majority, would let them, but these others always like attracting attention to themselves, and the animal provides them with a welcome pretext. If they could and if they dared, they would long ago have enticed the animal to come yet closer to them, so that they might be more frightened than ever. But in reality the animal is not at all eager to approach them,

mert sich, wenn es nicht angegriffen wird, um sie ebensowenig wie um die Männer, am liebsten würde es wahrscheinlich in der Verborgenheit bleiben, in der es in den Zeiten außerhalb des Gottesdienstes lebt, offenbar in irgendeinem Mauerloch, das wir noch nicht entdeckt haben. Erst wenn man zu beten anfängt, erscheint es, erschreckt durch den Lärm. Will es sehen, was geschehen ist, will es wachsam bleiben, will es frei sein, fähig zur Flucht? Vor Angst läuft es hervor, aus Angst macht es seine Kapriolen und wagt sich nicht zurückzuziehen, bis der Gottesdienst zu Ende ist. Die Höhe bevorzugt es natürlich deshalb, weil es dort am sichersten ist, und die besten Laufmöglichkeiten hat es auf dem Gitter und dem Mauervorsprung, aber es ist keineswegs immer dort, manchmal steigt es auch tiefer zu den Männern hinab, der Vorhang der Bundeslade wird von einer glänzenden Messingstange getragen, die scheint das Tier zu locken, oft genug schleicht es hin, dort aber ist es immer ruhig, nicht einmal wenn es dort knapp bei der Bundeslade ist, kann man sagen, daß es stört, mit seinen blanken, immer offenen, vielleicht lidlosen Augen scheint es die Gemeinde anzusehen, sieht aber gewiß niemanden an, sondern blickt nur den Gefahren entgegen, von denen es sich bedroht fühlt.

In dieser Hinsicht schien es, wenigstens bis vor kurzem, nicht viel verständiger als unsere Frauen. Was für Gefahren hat es denn zu fürchten? Wer beabsichtigt ihm etwas zu tun? Lebt es denn nicht seit vielen Jahren völlig sich selbst überlassen? Die Männer kümmern sich nicht um seine Anwesenheit, und die Mehrzahl

54

so long as it is left alone it takes just as little notice of them as of the men, and probably what it would like best would be to remain in the hiding place where it lives in the periods between the services, evidently some hole in the wall that we have not yet discovered. It is only when prayers begin that it appears, startled by the noise. Does it want to see what has happened? Does it want to remain on the alert? Does it want to be in the open, ready to take flight? It is in terror that it comes running out, it is in terror that it performs its capers, and it does not dare to withdraw until divine service is at an end. It naturally prefers being high up because that is where it is safest, and the places where it can run best are the lattice and the ledge, but it does not always stay there, sometimes too it climbs down farther towards the men; the curtain of the Ark of the Covenant hangs from a shining brass rod, and this seems to attract the animal, it quite often creeps towards it, but when it is there it is always quiet, not even when it is right up close to the Ark can it be said to be causing a disturbance, it seems to be gazing at the congregation with its bright, unwinking, and perhaps lidless eyes, but it is certainly not looking at anybody, it is only facing the dangers by which it feels itself threatened.

In this respect it seemed, at least until recently, to be not much more intelligent than our women. What dangers has it to fear, anyway? Who intends it any harm? Has it not been left entirely to itself for many years? The men take no notice of its presence, and the majority of the women would probably be miserable if

der Frauen wäre wahrscheinlich unglücklich, wenn es verschwände. Und da es das einzige Tier im Haus ist, hat es also überhaupt keinen Feind. Das hätte es nachgerade im Laufe der Jahre schon durchschauen können. Und der Gottesdienst mit seinem Lärm mag ja für das Tier sehr erschreckend sein, aber er wiederholt sich doch in bescheidenem Ausmaß jeden Tag und gesteigert an den Festtagen, immer regelmäßig und ohne Unterbrechung; auch das ängstlichste Tier hätte sich schon daran gewöhnen können, besonders, wenn es sieht, daß es nicht etwa der Lärm von Verfolgern ist, sondern ein Lärm, den es gar nicht begreift. Und doch diese Angst. Ist es die Erinnerung an längst vergangene oder die Vorahnung künftiger Zeiten? Weiß dieses alte Tier vielleicht mehr als die drei Generationen, die jeweils in der Synagoge versammelt sind?

Vor vielen Jahren, so erzählt man, soll man wirklich versucht haben, das Tier zu vertreiben. Es ist ja möglich, daß es wahr ist, wahrscheinlicher aber ist es, daß es sich nur um erfundene Geschichten handelt. Nachweisbar allerdings ist, daß man damals vom religionsgesetzlichen Standpunkt aus die Frage untersucht hat, ob man ein solches Tier im Gotteshause dulden darf. Man holte die Gutachten verschiedener berühmter Rabbiner ein, die Ansichten waren geteilt, die Mehrheit war für die Vertreibung und Neueinweihung des Gotteshauses. Aber es war leicht, von der Ferne zu dekretieren, in Wirklichkeit war es ja unmöglich, das Tier zu fangen, und deshalb auch unmöglich, es zu vertreiben. Denn nur, wenn man

it were to disappear. And since it is the only animal in the building, it has no enemy of any kind. This is something it really ought to have come to realize in the course of the years. And though divine service, with all its noise, may be very frightening for the animal, still, it does recur, on a modest scale daily and on a grander scale during the festivals, always regularly and without ever a break; and so even the most timid of animals could by now have got used to it, particularly when it sees that this is not the noise of pursuers, but some noise that it cannot understand at all. And yet there is this terror. Is it the memory of times long past or the premonition of times to come? Does this old animal perhaps know more than the three generations of those who are gathered together in the synagogue?

Many years ago, so it is recounted, attempts were really made to drive the animal away. It is possible, of course, that this is true, but it is more likely that such stories are mere inventions. There is evidence, however, that at that time the question whether the presence of such an animal might be tolerated in the house of God was investigated from the point of view of the Law and the Commandments. Opinions were sought from various celebrated rabbis, views were divided, the majority were for the expulsion of the animal and a reconsecration of the house of God. But it was easy to issue decrees from afar, in reality it was simply impossible to catch the animal, and hence it was also impossible to drive it out for good. For only if one could have caught it and taken it a long distance away

es gefangen und weit fortgeschafft hätte, hätte man die annähernde Sicherheit haben können, es los zu sein. Vor vielen Jahren, so erzählt man, soll man wirklich noch versucht haben, das Tier zu vertreiben. Der Tempeldiener will sich erinnern, daß sein Großvater, der auch Tempeldiener gewesen ist, mit Vorliebe davon erzählte. Dieser Großvater habe als kleiner Junge öfters von der Unmöglichkeit gehört, das Tier loszuwerden, da habe ihn, der ein ausgezeichneter Kletterer war, der Ehrgeiz nicht ruhen lassen, an einem hellen Vormittag, an dem die ganze Synagoge mit allen Winkeln und Verstecken im Sonnenlicht offen dalag, habe er sich hineingeschlichen, ausgerüstet mit einem Strick, einer Steinschleuder und einem Krummstock. . . .

could one have had anything approximating to a certainty of being rid of it.

Many years ago, so it is recounted, attempts were really still made to drive the animal away. The beadle of the synagogue says he remembers how his grandfather, who was also beadle, liked to tell the story. As a small boy his grandfather had frequently heard talk about the impossibility of getting rid of the animal, and so, fired by ambition and being an excellent climber, one bright morning when the whole synagogue, with all its nooks and crannies, lay open in the sunlight, he had sneaked in, armed with a rope, a catapult, and a crookhandled stick. . . .

"Vor dem Gesetz steht ein Türhüter. Zu diesem Türhüter kommt ein Mann vom Lande und bittet um Eintritt in das Gesetz. Aber der Türhüter sagt, dass er ihm jetzt den Eintritt nicht gewähren könne. Der Mann überlegt und fragt dann, ob er also später werde eintreten dürfen. 'Es ist möglich,' sagt der Türhüter, 'jetzt aber nicht.' Da das Tor zum Gesetz offensteht wie immer und der Türhüter beiseite tritt, bückt sich der Mann, um durch das Tor in das Innere zu sehen. Als der Türhüter das merkt, lacht er und sagt: 'Wenn es dich so lockt, versuche es doch, trotz meines Verbotes hineinzugehen. Merke aber: Ich bin mächtig. Und ich bin nur der unterste Türhüter. Von Saal zu Saal stehen aber Türhüter, einer mächtiger als der andere. Schon den Anblick des dritten kann nicht einmal ich mehr ertragen.' Solche Schwierigkeiten hat der Mann vom Lande nicht erwartet; das Gesetz soll doch jedem und immer zugänglich sein, denkt er, aber als er jetzt den Türhüter in seinem Pelzmantel genauer ansieht, seine grosse Spitznase, den langen, dünnen, schwarzen tatarischen Bart, entschliesst er sich, doch lieber zu warten, bis er die Erlaubnis zum Eintritt bekommt. Der Türhüter gibt ihm einen Schemel und lässt ihn seitwärts von der Tür sich niedersetzen. Dort sitzt er Tage und Jahre. Er macht viele Versuche, eingelassen zu werden, und ermüdet den Türhüter durch seine Bitten. Der Türhüter stellt öfters kleine Verhöre mit ihm an, fragt ihn über seine Heimat aus

"Before the Law stands a doorkeeper on guard. To this doorkeeper there comes a man from the country who begs for admittance to the Law. But the doorkeeper says that he cannot admit the man at the moment. The man, on reflection, asks if he will be allowed, then, to enter later. 'It is possible,' answers the doorkeeper, 'but not at this moment.' Since the door leading into the Law stands open as usual and the doorkeeper steps to one side, the man bends down to peer through the entrance. When the doorkeeper sees that, he laughs and says: 'If you are so strongly tempted, try to get in without my permission. But note that I am powerful. And I am only the lowest doorkeeper. From hall to hall keepers stand at every door, one more powerful than the other. Even the third of these has an aspect that even I cannot bear to look at.' These are difficulties which the man from the country has not expected to meet, the Law, he thinks, should be accessible to every man and at all times, but when he looks more closely at the doorkeeper in his furred robe, with his huge pointed nose and long, thin, Tartar beard, he decides that he had better wait until he gets permission to enter. The doorkeeper gives him a stool and lets him sit down at the side of the door. There he sits waiting for days and years. He makes many attempts to be allowed in and wearies the doorkeeper with his importunity. The doorkeeper often engages him in brief conversation, asking him about his home and about other matters, but the

und nach vielem anderen, es sind aber teilnahmslose Fragen, wie sie grosse Herren stellen, und zum Schlusse sagt er ihm immer wieder, dass er ihn noch nicht einlassen könne. Der Mann, der sich für seine Reise mit vielem ausgerüstet hat, verwendet alles, und sei es noch so wertvoll, um den Türhüter zu bestechen. Dieser nimmt zwar alles an, aber sagt dabei: 'Ich nehme es nur an, damit du nicht glaubst, etwas versäumt zu haben.' Während der vielen Jahre beobachtet der Mann den Türhüter fast ununterbrochen. Er vergisst die anderen Türhüter, und dieser erste scheint ihm das einzige Hindernis für den Eintritt in das Gesetz. Er verflucht den unglücklichen Zufall, in den ersten Jahren rücksichtslos und laut, später, als er alt wird, brummt er nur noch vor sich hin. Er wird kindisch, und da er in dem jahrelangen Studium des Türhüters auch die Flöhe in seinem Pelzkragen erkannt hat, bittet er auch die Flöhe, ihm zu helfen und den Türhüter umzustimmen. Schliesslich wird sein Augenlicht schwach, und er weiss nicht, ob es um ihn wirklich dunkler wird, oder ob ihn nur seine Augen täuschen. Wohl aber erkennt er jetzt im Dunkel einen Glanz, der unverlöschlich aus der Türe des Gesetzes bricht. Nun lebt er nicht mehr lange. Vor seinem Tode sammeln sich in seinem Kopfe alle Erfahrungen der ganzen Zeit zu einer Frage, die er bisher an den Türhüter noch nicht gestellt hat. Er winkt ihm zu, da er seinen erstarrenden Körper nicht mehr aufrichten kann. Der Türhüter muss sich tief zu ihm hinunterneigen, denn der Grössenunterschied hat sich sehr zuungunsten des Mannes verändert. 'Was

questions are put quite impersonally, as great men put questions, and always conclude with the statement that the man cannot be allowed to enter yet. The man, who has equipped himself with many things for his journey, parts with all he has, however valuable, in the hope of bribing the doorkeeper. The doorkeeper accepts it all, saying, however, as he takes each gift: 'I take this only to keep you from feeling that you have left something undone.' During all these long years the man watches the doorkeeper almost incessantly. He forgets about the other doorkeepers, and this one seems to him the only barrier between himself and the Law. In the first years he curses his evil fate aloud; later, as he grows old, he only mutters to himself. He grows childish, and since in his prolonged watch he has learned to know even the fleas in the doorkeeper's fur collar, he begs the very fleas to help him and to persuade the doorkeeper to change his mind. Finally his eyes grow dim and he does not know whether the world is really darkening around him or whether his eyes are only deceiving him. But in the darkness he can now perceive a radiance that streams immortally from the door of the Law. Now his life is drawing to a close. Before he dies, all that he has experienced during the whole time of his sojourn condenses in his mind into one question, which he has never yet put to the doorkeeper. He beckons the doorkeeper, since he can no longer raise his stiffening body. The doorkeeper has to bend far down to hear him, for the difference in size between them has increased very much to the man's disadvantage. 'What do you want to know now?' asks the doorkeeper, 'you are insatiable.'

willst du denn jetzt noch wissen?' fragt der Türhüter, 'du bist unersättlich.' 'Alle streben doch nach dem Gesetz,' sagt der Mann, 'wie kommt es, dass in den vielen Jahren niemand ausser mir Einlass verlangt hat?' Der Türhüter erkennt, dass der Mann schon an seinem Ende ist, und, um sein vergehendes Gehör noch zu erreichen, brüllt er ihn an: 'Hier konnte niemand sonst Einlass erhalten, denn dieser Eingang war nur für dich bestimmt. Ich gehe jetzt und schliesse ihn.' "

"Der Türhüter hat also den Mann getäuscht," sagte K. sofort, von der Geschichte sehr stark angezogen.

"Sei nicht übereilt," sagte der Geistliche, "übernimm nicht die fremde Meinung ungeprüft. Ich habe dir die Geschichte im Wortlaut der Schrift erzählt. Von Täuschung steht darin nichts."

"Es ist aber klar," sagte K., "und deine erste Deutung war ganz richtig. Der Türhüter hat die erlösende Mitteilung erst dann gemacht, als sie dem Manne nicht mehr helfen konnte."

"Er wurde nicht früher gefragt," sagte der Geistliche, "bedenke auch, dass er nur Türhüter war, und als solcher hat er seine Pflicht erfüllt."

"Warum glaubst du, dass er seine Pflicht erfüllt hat?" fragte K., "er hat sie nicht erfüllt. Seine Pflicht war es vielleicht, alle Fremden abzuwehren, diesen Mann aber, für den der Eingang bestimmt war, hätte er einlassen müssen."

"Du hast nicht genug Achtung vor der Schrift und veränderst die Geschichte," sagte der Geistliche. "Die Geschichte enthält über den Einlass ins Gesetz zwei wichtige Erklärungen des Türhüters, eine am Anfang,

'Everyone strives to attain the Law,' answers the man, 'how does it come about, then, that in all these years no one has come seeking admittance but me?' The doorkeeper perceives that the man is at the end of his strength and that his hearing is failing, so he bellows in his ear: 'No one but you could gain admittance through this door, since this door was intended only for you. I am now going to shut it.'"

"So the doorkeeper deluded the man," said K. immediately, strongly attracted by the story.

"Don't be too hasty," said the priest, "don't take over an opinion without testing it. I have told you the story in the very words of the scriptures. There's no mention of delusion in it."

"But it's clear enough," said K., "and your first interpretation of it was quite right. The doorkeeper gave the message of salvation to the man only when it could no longer help him."

"He was not asked the question any earlier," said the priest, "and you must consider, too, that he was only a doorkeeper, and as such he fulfilled his duty."

"What makes you think he fulfilled his duty?" asked K. "He didn't fulfill it. His duty might have been to keep all strangers away, but this man, for whom the door was intended, should have been let in."

"You have not enough respect for the written word and you are altering the story," said the priest. "The story contains two important statements made by the doorkeeper about admission to the Law, one at the beginning, the other at the end. The first statement is: that he cannot admit the man at the moment, and the

eine am Ende. Die eine Stelle lautet: dass er ihm jetzt den Eingang nicht gewähren könne, und die andere: dieser Eingang war nur für dich bestimmt. Bestände zwischen diesen beiden Erklärungen ein Widerspruch, dann hättest du recht, und der Türhüter hätte den Mann getäuscht. Nun besteht aber kein Widerspruch. Im Gegenteil, die erste Erklärung deutet sogar auf die zweite hin. Man könnte fast sagen, der Türhüter ging über seine Pflicht hinaus, indem er dem Mann eine zukünftige Möglichkeit des Einlasses in Aussicht stellte. Zu jener Zeit scheint es nur seine Pflicht gewesen zu sein, den Mann abzuweisen, und tatsächlich wundern sich viele Erklärer der Schrift darüber, dass der Türhüter jene Andeutung überhaupt gemacht hat, denn er scheint die Genauigkeit zu lieben und wacht streng über sein Amt. Durch viele Jahre verlässt er seinen Posten nicht und schliesst das Tor erst ganz zuletzt, er ist sich der Wichtigkeit seines Dienstes sehr bewusst, denn er sagt: 'Ich bin mächtig', er hat Ehrfurcht vor den Vorgesetzten, denn er sagt: 'Ich bin nur der unterste Türhüter,' er ist nicht geschwätzig, denn während der vielen Jahre stellt er nur, wie es heisst, 'teilnahmslose Fragen,' er ist nicht bestechlich, denn er sagt über ein Geschenk: 'Ich nehme es nur an, damit du nicht glaubst, etwas versäumt zu haben,' er ist, wo es um Pflichterfüllung geht, weder zu rühren noch zu erbittern, denn es heisst von dem Mann, 'er ermüdet den Türhüter durch seine Bitten,' schliesslich deutet auch sein Äusseres auf einen pedantischen Charakter hin, die grosse Spitznase und der lange, dünne, schwarze, tartarische Bart. Kann es einen

other is: that this door was intended only for the man. But there is no contradiction. The first statement, on the contrary, even implies the second. One could almost say that in suggesting to the man the possibility of future admittance the doorkeeper is exceeding his duty. At that moment his apparent duty is only to refuse admittance, and indeed many commentators are surprised that the suggestion should be made at all, since the doorkeeper appears to be a precisian with a stern regard for duty. He does not once leave his post during these many years, and he does not shut the door until the very last minute; he is conscious of the importance of his office, for he says: 'I am powerful'; he is respectful to his superiors, for he says: 'I am only the lowest doorkeeper'; he is not garrulous, for during all these years he puts only what are called 'impersonal questions'; he is not to be bribed, for he says in accepting a gift: 'I take this only to keep you from feeling that you have left something undone'; where his duty is concerned he is to be moved neither by pity nor rage, for we are told that the man 'wearied the doorkeeper with his importunity'; and finally even his external appearance hints at a pedantic character, the large, pointed nose and the long, thin, black Tartar beard. Could one imagine a more faithful doorkeeper? Yet the doorkeeper has other elements in his character which are likely to advantage anyone seeking admittance and which make it comprehensible enough that he should somewhat exceed his duty in suggesting the possibility of future admittance. For it cannot be denied that he is a little simple-minded and consequently a little conceited. Take the statements

pflichttreueren Türhüter geben? Nun mischen sich aber in den Türhüter noch andere Wesenzüge ein, die für den, der Einlass verlangt, sehr günstig sind, und welche es immerhin begreiflich machen, dass er in jener Andeutung einer zukünftigen Möglichkeit über seine Pflicht etwas hinausgehen konnte. Es ist nämlich nicht zu leugnen, dass er ein wenig einfältig und im Zusammenhang damit ein wenig eingebildet ist. Wenn auch seine Ausserungen über seine Macht und über die Macht der anderen Türhüter und über deren sogar für ihn unerträglichen Anblick—ich sage, wenn auch alle diese Ausserungen an sich richtig sein mögen, so zeigt doch die Art, wie er diese Ausserungen vorbringt, dass seine Auffassung durch Einfalt und Überhebung getrübt ist. Die Erklärer sagen hierzu: 'Richtiges Auffassen einer Sache und Missverstehen der gleichen Sache schliessen einander nicht vollständig aus.' Jedenfalls aber muss man annehmen, dass jene Einfalt und Überhebung, so geringfügig sie sich vielleicht auch äussern, doch die Bewachung des Eingangs schwächen, es sind Lücken im Charakter des Türhüters. Hierzu kommt noch, dass der Türhüter seiner Naturanlage nach freundlich zu sein scheint, er ist durchaus nicht immer Amtsperson. Gleich in den ersten Augenblicken macht er den Spass, dass er den Mann trotz dem ausdrücklich aufrechterhaltenen Verbot zum Eintritt einlädt, dann schickt er ihn nicht etwa fort, sondern gibt ihm, wie es heisst, einen Schemel und lässt ihn seitwärts von der Tür sich niedersetzen. Die Geduld, mit der er durch alle die Jahre die Bitten des Mannes erträgt, die kleinen Verhöre, die Annahme der Ge-

he makes about his power and the power of the other doorkeepers and their dreadful aspect which even he cannot bear to see—I hold that these statements may be true enough, but that the way in which he brings them out shows that his perceptions are confused by simpleness of mind and conceit. The commentators note in this connection: 'The right perception of any matter and a misunderstanding of the same matter do not wholly exclude each other.' One must at any rate assume that such simpleness and conceit, however sparingly indicated, are likely to weaken his defense of the door; they are breaches in the character of the doorkeeper. To this must be added the fact that the doorkeeper seems to be a friendly creature by nature, he is by no means always on his official dignity. In the very first moments he allows himself the jest of inviting the man to enter in spite of the strictly maintained veto against entry; then he does not, for instance, send the man away, but gives him, as we are told, a stool and lets him sit down beside the door. The patience with which he endures the man's appeals during so many years, the brief conversations, the acceptance of the gifts, the politeness with which he allows the man to curse loudly in his presence the fate for which he himself is responsible—all this lets us deduce certain motions of sympathy. Not every doorkeeper would have acted thus. And finally, in answer to a gesture of the man's he stoops low down to give him the chance of putting a last question. Nothing but mild impatience—the doorkeeper knows that this is the end of it all—is discernible in the words: 'You are insatiable.' Some push this mode of interpreta-

schenke, die Vornehmheit, mit der er es zulässt, dass der Mann neben ihm laut den unglücklichen Zufall verflucht, der den Türhüter hier aufgestellt hat—alles dieses lässt auf Regungen des Mitleids schliessen. Nicht jeder Türhüter hätte so gehandelt. Und schliesslich beugt er sich noch auf einen Wink hin tief zu dem Mann hinab, um ihm Gelegenheit zur letzten Frage zu geben. Nur eine schwache Ungeduld—der Türhüter weiss ja, dass alles zu Ende ist—spricht sich in den Worten aus: 'Du bist unersättlich.' Manche gehen sogar in dieser Art der Erklärung noch weiter und meinen, die Worte 'Du bist unersättlich,' drücken eine Art freundschaftlicher Bewunderung aus, die allerdings von Herablassung nicht frei ist. Jedenfalls schliesst sich so die Gestalt des Türhüters anders ab, als du glaubst."

"Du kennst die Geschichte genauer als ich und längere Zeit," sagte K. Sie schwiegen ein Weilchen. Dann sagte K.: "Du glaubst, also, der Mann wurde nicht getäuscht?"

"Missverstehe mich nicht," sagte der Geistliche, "ich zeige dir nur die Meinungen, die darüber bestehen. Du musst nicht zuviel auf Meinungen achten. Die Schrift ist unveränderlich, und die Meinungen sind oft nur ein Ausdruck der Verzweiflung darüber. In diesem Falle gibt es sogar eine Meinung, nach welcher gerade der Türhüter der Getäuschte ist."

"Das ist eine weitgehende Meinung," sagte K. "Wie wird sie begründet?"

"Die Begründung," antwortete der Geistliche, "geht von der Einfalt des Türhüters aus. Man sagt, dass er

tion even further and hold that these words express a kind of friendly admiration, though not without a hint of condescension. At any rate the figure of the doorkeeper can be said to come out very differently from what you fancied."

"You have studied the story more exactly and for a longer time than I have," said K. They were both silent for a little while. Then K. said: "So you think the man was not deluded?"

"Don't misunderstand me," said the priest, "I am only showing you the various opinions concerning that point. You must not pay too much attention to them. The scriptures are unalterable and the comments often enough merely express the commentator's bewilderment. In this case there even exists an interpretation which claims that the deluded person is really the doorkeeper."

"That's a far-fetched interpretation," said K. "On what is it based?"

"It is based," answered the priest, "on the simplemindedness of the doorkeeper. The argument is that he does not know the Law from inside, but he knows only the way that leads to it, where he patrols up and down. His ideas of the interior are assumed to be childish, and it is supposed that he himself is afraid of the other guardians whom he holds up as bogies before the man. Indeed, he fears them more than the man does, since the man is determined to enter after hearing about the dreadful guardians of the interior, while the doorkeeper has no desire to enter, at least not so far as we are told. Others again say that he must have been in the

das Innere des Gesetzes nicht kennt, sondern nur den Weg, den er vor dem Eingang immer wieder abgehen muss. Die Vorstellungen, die er von dem Innern hat, werden für kindlich gehalten, und man nimmt an, dass er das, wovor er dem Manne Furcht machen will, selbst fürchtet. Ja er fürchtet es mehr als der Mann, denn dieser will ja nichts anderes als eintreten, selbst als er von den schrecklichen Türhütern des Innern gehört hat, der Türhüter dagegen will nicht eintreten, wenigstens erfährt man nichts darüber. Andre sagen zwar, dass er bereits im Innern gewesen sein muss, denn er ist doch einmal in den Dienst des Gesetzes aufgenommen worden, und das könne nur im Innern geschehen sein. Darauf ist zu antworten, dass er wohl auch durch einen Ruf aus dem Innern zum Türhüter bestellt worden sein könne, und dass er zumindest tief im Innern nicht gewesen sein dürfte, da er doch schon den Anblick des dritten Türhüters nicht mehr ertragen kann. Ausserdem aber wird auch nicht berichtet, dass er während der vielen Jahre ausser der Bemerkung über die Türhüter irgend etwas von dem Innern erzählt hätte. Es könnte ihm verboten sein, aber auch vom Verbot hat er nichts erzählt. Aus alledem schliesst man, dass er über das Aussehen und die Bedeutung des Innern nichts weiss und sich darüber in Täuschung befindet. Aber auch über den Mann vom Lande soll er sich in Täuschung befinden, denn er ist diesem Mann untergeordnet und weiss es nicht. Dass er den Mann als einen Untergeordneten behandelt, erkennt man aus vielem, das dir noch erinnerlich sein dürfte. Dass er ihm aber tatsächlich untergeordnet ist, soll nach

72

interior already, since he is after all engaged in the service of the Law and can only have been appointed from inside. This is countered by arguing that he may have been appointed by a voice calling from the interior, and that anyhow he cannot have been far inside, since the aspect of the third doorkeeper is more than he can endure. Moreover, no indication is given that all these years he ever made any remarks showing a knowledge of the interior except for the one remark about the doorkeepers. He may have been forbidden to do so, but there is no mention of that either. On these grounds the conclusion is reached that he knows nothing about the aspect and significance of the interior, so that he is in a state of delusion. But he is deceived also about his relation to the man from the country, for he is subject to the man and does not know it. He treats the man instead as his own subordinate, as can be recognized from many details that must still be fresh in your mind. But, according to this view of the story, it is just as clearly indicated that he is really subordinated to the man. In the first place, a bondman is always subject to a free man. Now the man from the country is really free, he can go where he likes, it is only the Law that is closed to him, and access to the Law is forbidden him only by one individual, the doorkeeper. When he sits down on the stool by the side of the door and stays there for the rest of his life, he does it of his own free will; in the story there is no mention of any compulsion. But the doorkeeper is bound to his post by his very office, he does not dare strike out into the country, nor apparently may he go into the interior of the Law,

dieser Meinung ebenso deutlich hervorgehen. Vor allem ist der Freie dem Gebundenen übergeordnet: Nun ist der Mann tatsächlich frei, er kann hingehen, wohin er will, nur der Eingang in das Gesetz ist ihm verboten, und überdies nur von einem einzelnen, vom Türhüter. Wenn er sich auf den Schemel seitwärts vom Tor niedersetzt und dort sein Leben lang bleibt, so geschieht dies freiwillig, die Geschichte erzählt von keinem Zwang. Der Türhüter dagegen ist durch sein Amt an seinen Posten gebunden, er darf sich nicht auswärts entfernen, allem Anschein nach aber auch nicht in das Innere gehen, selbst wenn er es wollte. Ausserdem ist er zwar im Dienst des Gesetzes, dient aber nur für diesen Eingang, also auch nur für diesen Mann, für den dieser Eingang allein bestimmt ist. Auch aus diesem Grunde ist er ihm untergeordnet. Es ist anzunehmen, dass er durch viele Jahre, durch ein ganzes Mannesalter gewissermassen nur leeren Dienst geleistet hat, denn es wird gesagt, dass ein Mann kommt, also jemand im Mannesalter, dass also der Türhüter lange warten musste, ehe sich sein Zweck erfüllte, und zwar so lange warten musste, als es dem Mann beliebte, der doch freiwillig kam. Aber auch das Ende des Dienstes wird durch das Lebensende des Mannes bestimmt, bis zum Ende also bleibt er ihm untergeordnet. Und immer wieder wird betont, dass von alledem der Türhüter nichts zu wissen scheint. Daran wird aber nichts Auffälliges gesehen, denn nach dieser Meinung befindet sich der Türhüter noch in einer viel schwereren Täuschung, sie betrifft seinen Dienst. Zuletzt spricht er nämlich vom Eingang und

even should he wish to. Besides, although he is in the service of the Law, his service is confined to this one entrance; that is to say, he serves only this man for whom alone the entrance is intended. On that ground too he is subject to the man. One must assume that for many years, for as long as it takes a man to grow up to the prime of life, his service was in a sense empty formality, since he had to wait for a man to come, that is to say, someone in the prime of life, and so had to wait a long time before the purpose of his service could be fulfilled, and, moreover, had to wait on the man's pleasure, for the man came of his own free will. But the termination of his service also depends on the man's term of life, so that to the very end he is subject to the man. And it is emphasized throughout that the doorkeeper apparently realizes nothing of all this. That is not in itself remarkable, since according to this interpretation the doorkeeper is deceived in a much more important issue, affecting his very office. At the end, for example, he says regarding the entrance to the Law: 'I am now going to shut it,' but at the beginning of the story we are told that the door leading into the Law stands always open, and if it stands open always, that is to say, at all times, without reference to the life or death of the man, then the doorkeeper is incapable of closing it. There is some difference of opinions about the motive behind the doorkeeper's statement, whether he said he was going to close the door merely for the sake of giving an answer, or to emphasize his devotion to duty, or to bring the man into a state of grief and regret in his last moments. But there is no lack of agree-

sagt: 'Ich gehe jetzt und schliesse ihn,' aber am Anfang heisst es, dass das Tor zum Gesetz offensteht wie immer, steht es aber immer offen, immer, das heisst unabhängig von der Lebensdauer des Mannes, für den es bestimmt ist, dann wird es auch der Türhüter nicht schliessen können. Darüber gehen die Meinungen auseinander, ob der Türhüter mit der Ankündigung, dass er das Tor schliessen wird, nur eine Antwort geben oder seine Dienstpflicht betonen oder den Mann noch im letzten Augenblick in Reue und Trauer setzen will. Darin aber sind viele einig, dass er das Tor nicht wird schliessen können. Sie glauben sogar, dass er, wenigstens am Ende, auch in seinem Wissen dem Manne untergeordnet ist, denn dieser sieht den Glanz, der aus dem Eingang des Gesetzes bricht, während der Türhüter als solcher wohl mit dem Rücken zum Eingang steht und auch durch keine Äusserung zeigt, dass er eine Veränderung bemerkt hätte.''

"Das ist gut begründet," sagte K., der einzelne Stellen aus der Erklärung des Geistlichen halblaut für sich wiederholt hatte. "Es ist gut begründet, und ich glaube nun auch, dass der Türhüter getäuscht ist. Dadurch bin ich aber von meiner früheren Meinung nicht abgekommen, denn beide decken sich teilweise. Es ist unentscheidend, ob der Türhüter klar sieht oder getäuscht wird. Ich sagte, der Mann wird getäuscht. Wenn der Türhüter klar sieht, könnte man daran zweifeln, wenn der Türhüter aber getäuscht ist, dann muss sich seine Täuschung notwendig auf den Mann übertragen. Der Türhüter ist dann zwar kein Betrüger, aber so einfältig,

ment that the doorkeeper will not be able to shut the door. Many indeed profess to find that he is subordinate to the man even in wisdom, towards the end, at least, for the man sees the radiance that issues from the door of the Law while the doorkeeper in his official position must stand with his back to the door, nor does he say anything to show that he has perceived the change."

"That is well argued," said K., after repeating to himself in a low voice several passages from the priest's exposition. "It is well argued, and I am inclined to agree that the doorkeeper is deluded. But that has not made me abandon my former opinion, since both conclusions are to some extent compatible. Whether the doorkeeper is clear-sighted or deluded does not dispose of the matter. I said the man is deluded. If the doorkeeper is clear-sighted, one might have doubts about that, but if the doorkeeper himself is deluded, then his delusion must of necessity be communicated to the man. That makes the doorkeeper not, indeed, a swindler, but a creature so simple-minded that he ought to be dismissed at once from his office. You mustn't forget that the doorkeeper's delusions do himself no harm but do infinite harm to the man."

"There are objections to that," said the priest. "Many aver that the story confers no right on anyone to pass judgment on the doorkeeper. Whatever he may seem to us, he is yet a servant of the Law; that is, he belongs to the Law and as such is set beyond human judgment. In that case one dare not believe that the doorkeeper is subordinate to the man. Bound as he is by his service,

dass er sofort aus dem Dienst gejagt werden müsste. Du musst doch bedenken, dass die Täuschung, in der sich der Türhüter befindet, ihm nichts schadet, dem Mann aber tausendfach."

"Hier stösst du auf eine Gegenmeinung," sagte der Geistliche. "Manche sagen nämlich, dass die Geschichte niemandem ein Recht gibt, über den Türhüter zu urteilen. Wie es uns auch erscheinen mag, so ist er doch ein Diener des Gesetzes, also zum Gesetz gehörig, also dem menschlichen Urteil entrückt. Man darf dann auch nicht glauben, dass der Türhüter dem Manne untergeordnet ist. Durch seinen Dienst auch nur an den Eingang des Gesetzes gebunden zu sein, ist unvergleichlich mehr, als frei in der Welt zu leben. Der Mann kommt erst zum Gesetz, der Türhüter ist schon dort. Er ist vom Gesetz zum Dienst bestellt, an seiner Würdigkeit zu zweifeln, hiesse am Gesetz zweifeln."

"Mit dieser Meinung stimme ich nicht überein," sagte K. kopfschüttelnd, "denn wenn man sich ihr anschliesst, muss man alles, was der Türhüter sagt, für wahr halten. Dass das aber nicht möglich ist, hast du ja selbst ausführlich begründet."

"Nein," sagte der Geistliche, "man muss nicht alles für wahr halten, man muss es nur für notwendig halten."

"Trübselige Meinung," sagte K. "Die Lüge wird zur Weltordnung gemacht."

even at the door of the Law, he is incomparably freer than anyone at large in the world. The man is only seeking the Law, the doorkeeper is already attached to it. It is the Law that has placed him at his post; to doubt his integrity is to doubt the Law itself."

"I don't agree with that point of view," said K. shaking his head, "for if one accepts it, one must accept as true everything the doorkeeper says. But you yourself have sufficiently proved how impossible it is to do that."

"No," said the priest, "it is not necessary to accept everything as true, one must only accept it as necessary."

"A melancholy conclusion," said K. "It turns lying into a universal principle."

Ich überlief den ersten Wächter. Nachträglich erschrak ich, lief wieder zurück und sagte dem Wächter: »Ich bin hier durchgelaufen, während du abgewendet warst.« Der Wächter sah vor sich hin und schwieg. »Ich hätte es wohl nicht tun sollen«, sagte ich. Der Wächter schwieg noch immer. »Bedeutet dein Schweigen die Erlaubnis zu passieren?« . . .

DAS KOMMEN DES MESSIAS

Der Messias wird kommen, sobald der zügelloseste Individualismus des Glaubens möglich ist—, niemand diese Möglichkeit vernichtet, niemand die Vernichtung duldet, also die Gräber sich öffnen. Das ist vielleicht auch die christliche Lehre, sowohl in der tatsächlichen Aufzeigung des Beispieles, dem nachgefolgt werden soll, eines individualistischen Beispieles, als auch in der symbolischen Aufzeigung der Auferstehung des Mittlers im einzelnen Menschen.

Der Messias wird erst kommen, wenn er nicht mehr nötig sein wird, er wird erst einen Tag nach seiner Ankunft kommen, er wird nicht am letzten Tag kommen, sondern am allerletzten.

THE WATCHMAN

I ran past the first watchman. Then I was horrified, ran back again and said to the watchman: "I ran through here while you were looking the other way." The watchman gazed ahead of him and said nothing. "I suppose I really oughtn't to have done it," I said. The watchman still said nothing. "Does your silence indicate permission to pass?" . . .

THE COMING OF THE MESSIAH

The Messiah will come as soon as the most unbridled individualism of faith becomes possible—when there is no one to destroy this possibility and no one to suffer its destruction; hence the graves will open themselves. This, perhaps, is Christian doctrine too, applying as much to the actual presentation of the example to be emulated, which is an individualistic example, as to the symbolic presentation of the resurrection of the Mediator in the single individual.

The Messiah will come only when he is no longer necessary; he will come only on the day after his arrival; he will come, not on the last day, but on the very last.

Von Prometheus berichten vier Sagen:

Nach der ersten wurde er, weil er die Götter an die Menschen verraten hatte, am Kaukasus festgeschmiedet, und die Götter schickten Adler, die von seiner immer wachsenden Leber frassen.

Nach der zweiten drückte sich Prometheus im Schmerz vor den zuhackenden Schnäbeln immer tiefer in den Felsen, bis er mit ihm eins wurde.

Nach der dritten wurde in den Jahrtausenden sein Verrat vergessen, die Götter vergassen, die Adler, er selbst.

Nach der vierten wurde man des grundlos Gewordenen müde. Die Götter wurden müde, die Adler wurden müde, die Wunde schloss sich müde.

Blieb das unerklärliche Felsgebirge.—Die Sage versucht, das Unerklärliche zu erklären. Da sie aus einem Wahrheitsgrund kommt, muss sie wieder im Unerklärlichen enden.

There are four legends concerning Prometheus:

According to the first, he was clamped to a rock in the Caucasus for betraying the secrets of the gods to men, and the gods sent eagles to feed on his liver, which was perpetually renewed.

According to the second, Prometheus, goaded by the pain of the tearing beaks, pressed himself deeper and deeper into the rock until he became one with it.

According to the third, his treachery was forgotten in the course of thousands of years, the gods forgotten, the eagles, he himself forgotten.

According to the fourth, every one grew weary of the meaningless affair. The gods grew weary, the eagles grew weary, the wound closed wearily.

There remained the inexplicable mass of rock.—The legend tried to explain the inexplicable. As it came out of a substratum of truth it had in turn to end in the inexplicable.

Poseidon sass an seinem Arbeitstisch und rechnete. Die Verwaltung aller Gewässer gab ihm unendliche Arbeit. Er hätte Hilfskräfte haben können, wie viel er wollte, und er hatte auch sehr viele, aber da er sein Amt sehr ernst nahm, rechnete er alles noch einmal durch und so halfen ihm die Hilfskräfte wenig. Man kann nicht sagen, dass ihn die Arbeit freute, er führte sie eigentlich nur aus, weil sie ihm auferlegt war, ja er hatte sich schon oft um fröhlichere Arbeit, wie er sich ausdrückte, beworben, aber immer, wenn man ihm dann verschiedene Vorschläge machte, zeigte es sich, dass ihm doch nichts so zusagte, wie sein bisheriges Amt. Es war auch sehr schwer, etwas anderes für ihn zu finden. Man konnte ihm doch unmöglich etwa ein bestimmtes Meer zuweisen; abgesehen davon, dass auch hier die rechnerische Arbeit nicht kleiner, sondern nur kleinlicher war, konnte der grosse Poseidon doch immer nur eine beherrschende Stellung bekommen. Und bot man ihm eine Stellung ausserhalb des Wassers an, wurde ihm schon von der Vorstellung übel, sein göttlicher Atem geriet in Unordnung, sein eherner Brustkorb schwankte. Übrigens nahm man seine Beschwerden nicht eigentlich ernst; wenn ein Mächtiger quält, muss man ihm auch in der aussichtslosesten Angelegenheit scheinbar nachzugeben versuchen; an eine wirkliche Enthebung Poseidons von seinem Amt dachte niemand, seit Urbeginn war er zum Gott der Meere bestimmt worden und dabei musste es bleiben.

Poseidon sat at his desk, doing figures. The administration of all the waters gave him endless work. He could have had assistants, as many as he wanted—and he did have very many—but since he took his job very seriously, he would in the end go over all the figures and calculations himself, and thus his assistants were of little help to him. It cannot be said that he enjoyed his work; he did it only because it had been assigned to him; in fact, he had already filed many petitions for—as he put it—more cheerful work, but every time the offer of something different was made to him it would turn out that nothing suited him quite as well as his present position. And anyhow it was quite difficult to find something different for him. After all, it was impossible to assign him to a particular sea; aside from the fact that even then the work with figures would not become less but only pettier, the great Poseidon could in any case occupy only an executive position. And when a job away from the water was offered to him he would get sick at the very prospect, his divine breathing would become troubled and his brazen chest begin to tremble. Besides, his complaints were not really taken seriously; when one of the mighty is vexatious the appearance of an effort must be made to placate him, even when the case is most hopeless. In actuality a shift of posts was unthinkable for Poseidon—he had been appointed God of the Sea in the beginning, and that he had to remain.

Am meisten ärgerte er sich—und dies verursachte hauptsächlich seine Unzufriedenheit mit dem Amt— wenn er von den Vorstellungen hörte, die man sich von ihm machte, wie er etwa immerfort mit dem Dreizack durch die Fluten kutschiere. Unterdessen sass er hier in der Tiefe des Weltmeeres und rechnete ununterbrochen, hie und da eine Reise zu Jupiter war die einzige Unterbrechung der Eintönigkeit, eine Reise übrigens, von der er meistens wütend zurückkehrte. So hatte er die Meere kaum gesehen, nur flüchtig beim eiligen Aufstieg zum Olymp, und niemals wirklich durchfahren. Er pflegte zu sagen, er warte damit bis zum Weltuntergang, dann werde sich wohl noch ein stiller Augenblick ergeben, wo er knapp vor dem Ende nach Durchsicht der letzten Rechnung noch schnell eine kleine Rundfahrt werde machen können.

Poseidon wurde überdrüssig seiner Meere. Der Dreizack entfiel ihm. Still sass er an felsiger Küste und eine von seiner Gegenwart betäubte Möve zog schwankende Kreise um sein Haupt.

What irritated him most—and it was this that was chiefly responsible for his dissatisfaction with his job—was to hear of the conceptions formed about him: how he was always riding about through the tides with his trident. When all the while he sat here in the depths of the world-ocean, doing figures uninterruptedly, with now and then a trip to Jupiter as the only break in the monotony—a trip, moreover, from which he usually returned in a rage. Thus he had hardly seen the sea—had seen it but fleetingly in the course of hurried ascents to Olympus, and he had never actually travelled around it. He was in the habit of saying that what he was waiting for was the fall of the world; then, probably, a quiet moment would yet be granted in which, just before the end and after having checked the last row of figures, he would be able to make a quick little tour.

Poseidon became bored with his sea. He let fall his trident. Silently he sat on the rocky coast and a gull, dazed by his presence, described wavering circles around his head.

DAS SCHWEIGEN DER SIRENEN

Beweis dessen, dass auch unzulängliche, ja kindische
Mittel zur Rettung dienen können:

Um sich vor den Sirenen zu bewahren, stopfte sich
Odysseus Wachs in die Ohren und liess sich am Mast
festschmieden. Ähnliches hätten natürlich seit jeher alle
Reisenden tun können, ausser denen, welche die
Sirenen schon aus der Ferne verlockten, aber es war
in der ganzen Welt bekannt, dass dies unmöglich helfen konnte. Der Sang der Sirenen durchdrang alles,
und die Leidenschaft der Verführten hätte mehr als
Ketten und Mast gesprengt. Daran aber dachte Odysseus nicht, obwohl er davon vielleicht gehört hatte.
Er vertraute vollständig der Handvoll Wachs und dem
Gebinde Ketten, und in unschuldiger Freude über
seine Mittelchen fuhr er den Sirenen entgegen.

Nun haben aber die Sirenen eine noch schrecklichere
Waffe als den Gesang, nämlich ihr Schweigen. Es ist
zwar nicht geschehen, aber vielleicht denkbar, dass sich
jemand vor ihrem Gesang gerettet hätte, vor ihrem
Schweigen gewiss nicht. Dem Gefühl, aus eigener
Kraft sie besiegt zu haben, der daraus folgenden alles
fortreissenden Überhebung kann nichts Irdisches
widerstehen.

Und tatsächlich sangen, als Odysseus kam, die
gewaltigen Sängerinnen nicht, sei es, dass sie glaubten,
diesem Gegner könne nur noch das Schweigen beikom-
men, sei es, dass der Anblick der Glückseligkeit im
Gesicht des Odysseus, der an nichts anderes als an

88

Proof that inadequate, even childish measures, may serve to rescue one from peril.

To protect himself from the Sirens Ulysses stopped his ears with wax and had himself bound to the mast of his ship. Naturally any and every traveller before him could have done the same, except those whom the Sirens allured even from a great distance; but it was known to all the world that such things were of no help whatever. The song of the Sirens could pierce through everything, and the longing of those they seduced would have broken far stronger bonds than chains and masts. But Ulysses did not think of that, although he had probably heard of it. He trusted absolutely to his handful of wax and his fathom of chain, and in innocent elation over his little stratagem sailed out to meet the Sirens.

Now the Sirens have a still more fatal weapon than their song, namely their silence. And though admittedly such a thing has never happened, still it is conceivable that someone might possibly have escaped from their singing; but from their silence certainly never. Against the feeling of having triumphed over them by one's own strength, and the consequent exaltation that bears down everything before it, no earthly powers could have remained intact.

And when Ulysses approached them the potent songstresses actually did not sing, whether because they thought that this enemy could be vanquished only by

Wachs und Ketten dachte, sie allen Gesang vergessen liess.

Odysseus aber, um es so auszudrücken, hörte ihr Schweigen nicht, er glaubte, sie sängen, und nur er sei behütet, es zu hören. Flüchtig sah er zuerst die Wendungen ihrer Hälse, das tiefe Atmen, die tränenvollen Augen, den halb geöffneten Mund, glaubte aber, dies gehöre zu den Arien, die ungehört um ihn verklangen. Bald aber glitt alles an seinen in die Ferne gerichteten Blicken ab, die Sirenen verschwanden förmlich vor seiner Entschlossenheit, und gerade als er ihnen am nächsten war, wusste er nichts mehr von ihnen.

Sie aber—schöner als jemals—streckten und drehten sich, liessen das schaurige Haar offen im Winde wehen und spannten die Krallen frei auf den Felsen. Sie wollten nicht mehr verführen, nur noch den Abglanz vom grossen Augenpaar des Odysseus wollten sie so lange als möglich erhaschen.

Hätten die Sirenen Bewusstsein, sie wären damals vernichtet worden. So aber blieben sie, nur Odysseus ist ihnen entgangen.

Es wird übrigens noch ein Anhang hierzu überliefert. Odysseus, sagt man, war so listenreich, war ein solcher Fuchs, dass selbst die Schicksalsgöttin nicht in sein Innerstes dringen konnte. Vielleicht hat er, obwohl das mit Menschenverstand nicht mehr zu begreifen ist, wirklich gemerkt, dass die Sirenen schwiegen, und hat ihnen und den Göttern den obigen Scheinvorgang nur gewissermassen als Schild entgegengehalten.

their silence, or because the look of bliss on the face of Ulysses, who was thinking of nothing but his wax and his chains, made them forget their singing.

But Ulysses, if one may so express it, did not hear their silence; he thought they were singing and that he alone did not hear them. For a fleeting moment he saw their throats rising and falling, their breasts lifting, their eyes filled with tears, their lips half-parted, but believed that these were accompaniments to the airs which died unheard around him. Soon, however, all this faded from his sight as he fixed his gaze on the distance, the Sirens literally vanished before his resolution, and at the very moment when they were nearest to him he knew of them no longer.

But they—lovelier than ever—stretched their necks and turned, let their cold hair flutter free in the wind, and forgetting everything clung with their claws to the rocks. They no longer had any desire to allure; all that they wanted was to hold as long as they could the radiance that fell from Ulysses' great eyes.

If the Sirens had possessed consciousness they would have been annihilated at that moment. But they remained as they had been; all that had happened was that Ulysses had escaped them.

A codicil to the foregoing has also been handed down. Ulysses, it is said, was so full of guile, was such a fox, that not even the goddess of fate could pierce his armor. Perhaps he had really noticed, although here the human understanding is beyond its depths, that the Sirens were silent, and opposed the afore-mentioned pretense to them and the gods merely as a sort of shield.

DIE SIRENEN

Das sind die verführerischen Nachtstimmen; die
Sirenen haben auch so gesungen, man tut ihnen
unrecht, wenn man glaubt, dass sie verführen wollten,
sie wussten, dass sie Krallen hatten und keinen frucht-
baren Schoss, darüber klagten sie laut, sie konnten
nicht dafür, dass die Klage so schön klang.

LEOPARDEN IN TEMPEL

Leoparden brechen in den Tempel ein und saufen die
Opferkrüge leer; das wiederholt sich immer wieder;
schließlich kann man es vorausberechnen, und es wird
ein Teil der Zeremonie.

THE SIRENS

These are the seductive voices of the night; the Sirens, too, sang that way. It would be doing them an injustice to think that they wanted to seduce; they knew they had claws and sterile wombs, and they lamented this aloud. They could not help it if their laments sounded so beautiful.

LEOPARDS IN THE TEMPLE

Leopards break into the temple and drink to the dregs what is in the sacrificial pitchers; this is repeated over and over again; finally it can be calculated in advance, and it becomes a part of the ceremony.

ALEXANDER DER GROSSE

Es wäre denkbar, dass Alexander der Grosse trotz den kriegerischen Erfolgen seiner Jugend, trotz dem ausgezeichneten Heer, das er ausgebildet hatte, trotz den auf Veränderung der Welt gerichteten Kräften, die er in sich fühlte, am Hellespont stehen geblieben und ihn nie überschritten hätte, und zwar nicht aus Furcht, nicht aus Unentschlossenheit, nicht aus Willensschwäche, sondern aus Erdenschwere.

DIOGENES

In meinem Fall kann man sich drei Kreise denken, einen innersten A, dann B, dann C. Der Kern A erklärt dem B, warum dieser Mensch sich quälen und sich mißtrauen muß, warum er verzichten muß, warum er nicht leben darf. (War nicht zum Beispiel Diogenes in diesem Sinne schwerkrank? Wer von uns wäre nicht glücklich unter dem strahlenden Blick Alexanders gewesen? Diogenes aber bat ihn verzweifelt, die Sonne freizugeben. Dieses Faß war von Gespenstern voll.) C, dem handelnden Menschen, wird nicht mehr erklärt, ihm befiehlt bloß schrecklich B; C handelt unter strengstem Druck, aber mehr in Angst, als in Verständnis, er vertraut, er glaubt, daß A dem B alles erklärt und B alles richtig verstanden hat.

94

It is conceivable that Alexander the Great, in spite of the martial successes of his early days, in spite of the excellent army that he had trained, in spite of the power he felt within him to change the world, might have remained standing on the bank of the Hellespont and never have crossed it, and not out of fear, not out of indecision, not out of infirmity of will, but because of the mere weight of his own body.

DIOGENES

In my case one can imagine three circles, an innermost one, A, then B, then C. The core A explains to B why this man must torment and mistrust himself, why he must renounce, why he must not live. (Was not Diogenes, for instance, gravely ill in this sense? Which of us would not have been happy under Alexander's radiant gaze? But Diogenes frantically begged him to move out of the way of the sun. That tub was full of ghosts.) To C, the active man, no explanations are given, he is merely terribly ordered about by B; C acts under the most severe pressure, but more in fear than in understanding, he trusts, he believes, that A explains everything to B and that B has understood everything rightly.

Wir haben einen neuen Advokaten, den Dr. Bucephalus. In seinem Äussern erinnert wenig an die Zeit, da er noch Streitross Alexanders von Mazedonien war. Wer allerdings mit den Umständen vertraut ist, bemerkt einiges. Doch sah ich letzthin auf der Freitreppe selbst einen ganz einfältigen Gerichtsdiener mit dem Fachblick des kleinen Stammgastes der Wettrennen den Advokaten bestaunen, als dieser, hoch die Schenkel hebend, mit auf dem Marmor aufklingendem Schritt von Stufe zu Stufe stieg.

Im allgemeinen billigt das Barreau die Aufnahme des Bucephalus. Mit erstaunlicher Einsicht sagt man sich, dass Bucephalus bei der heutigen Gesellschaftsordnung in einer schwierigen Lage ist, und dass er deshalb, sowie auch wegen seiner weltgeschichtlichen Bedeutung, jedenfalls Entgegenkommen verdient. Heute—das kann niemand leugnen—gibt es keinen grossen Alexander. Zu morden verstehen zwar manche; auch an der Geschicklichkeit, mit der Lanze über den Bankettisch hinweg den Freund zu treffen, fehlt es nicht; und vielen ist Mazedonien zu eng, sodass sie Philipp, den Vater, verfluchen—aber niemand, niemand kann nach Indien führen. Schon damals waren Indiens Tore unerreichbar, aber ihre Richtung war durch das Königsschwert bezeichnet. Heute sind die Tore ganz anderswohin und weiter und höher vertragen; niemand zeigt die Richtung; viele halten Schwerter; aber nur, um mit ihnen zu fuchteln, und der Blick, der ihnen folgen will, verwirrt sich.

We have a new attorney, Dr. Bucephalus. There is little about his external appearance to remind one of the time when he was still Alexander of Macedon's charger. But anyone familiar with such matters can still notice something. Did I not just lately see even a quite simple court attendant stare at the lawyer with the professional eye of a modest racetrack follower as the latter, lifting his legs high, mounted the outside stairs step by step, with a tread that made the marble ring?

The bar has in general approved of Bucephalus' admission. They tell themselves, with amazing insight, that Bucephalus' position under our present social system is a difficult one and that he therefore—and also because of his world-historical significance—deserves to be met halfway. Today, as no one can deny, there is no Alexander the Great. Many, of course, still know how to murder; nor is there any lack of skill at stabbing your friend over the banquet table with a lance; and for many Macedonia is too narrow, so that they curse Philip, the father—but no one, no one can lead us to India. Even in those days India's gates were unattainable, but their direction was designated by the royal sword. Today the gates have been shifted elsewhere and higher and farther away; nobody points out their direction; many hold swords, but only to flourish them, and the glance that tries to follow them becomes confused.

Therefore it may really be best, perhaps, to do as

Vielleicht ist es deshalb wirklich das beste, sich, wie es Bucephalus getan hat, in die Gesetzbücher zu versenken. Frei, unbedrückt die Seiten von den Lenden des Reiters, bei stiller Lampe, fern dem Getöse der Alexanderschlacht, liest und wendet er die Blätter unserer alten Bücher.

Bucephalus has done and bury oneself in the law books. Free, his flanks unpressed by the thighs of a rider, under a quiet lamp, far from the din of Alexander's battles, he reads and turns the pages of our old books.

Es kamen einige Leute zu mir und baten mich, eine
Stadt für sie zu bauen. Ich sagte, sie wären viel zu
wenige, sie hätten Raum in einem Haus, für sie
würde ich keine Stadt bauen. Sie aber sagten, es
würden noch andere nachkommen und es seien doch
Eheleute unter ihnen, die Kinder zu erwarten hätten,
auch müßte die Stadt nicht auf einmal gebaut, sondern nur im Umriß festgelegt und nach und nach
ausgeführt werden. Ich fragte, wo sie die Stadt aufgebaut haben wollten, sie sagten, sie würden mir den
Ort gleich zeigen. Wir gingen den Fluß entlang, bis
wir zu einer genug hohen, zum Fluß hin steilen,
sonst aber sanft sich abflachenden und sehr breiten
Erhebung kamen. Sie sagten, dort oben wollten sie
die Stadt gebaut haben. Es war dort nur schütterer
Graswuchs, keine Bäume, das gefiel mir, der Abfall
zum Fluß schien mir aber zu steil und ich machte
sie darauf aufmerksam. Sie aber sagten, das sei kein
Schaden, die Stadt werde sich ja auf den andern
Abhängen ausdehnen und genug andere Zugänge
zum Wasser haben, auch würden sich vielleicht im
Laufe der Zeiten Mittel finden, den steilen Abhang
irgendwie zu überwinden, jedenfalls solle das kein
Hindernis für die Gründung der Stadt an diesem
Orte sein. Auch seien sie jung und stark und könnten
mit Leichtigkeit den Abhang erklettern, was sie mir
gleich zeigen wollten. Sie taten es, wie Eidechsen
schwangen sich ihre Körper zwischen den Rissen des

Some people came to me and asked me to build a city for them. I said there were far too few of them, there would be room enough for them in one house, I was not going to build any city for them. But they said there would be yet others coming along and that there were, after all, married people among them who were expecting children, nor need the city be built all at once, but only the ground plan established and the rest carried out bit by bit. I asked where they wanted to have the city built; they said they would show me the place in a moment. We went along the river until we came to a fairly high broad hill, steep on the side next to the river but otherwise sloping away gently. They said up there was where they wanted to have the city built. There was nothing there but thin-growing grass, and no trees, which suited me, but the drop to the river seemed too steep to me and I drew their attention to this. They said, however, that there was no harm in this, the city would, after all, extend along the other slopes and would have enough other means of access to the water, and besides, in the course of time ways would perhaps be found of somehow coping with the steep cliff; in any case, that was not to be any obstacle to founding a city on this spot. Besides, they said, they were young and strong and could easily climb up the cliff, which they said they would demonstrate to me at once. They did so; like lizards their bodies darted upwards among the crevices in the rock,

Felsens hinauf, bald waren sie oben. Ich ging auch hinauf und fragte sie, warum sie gerade hier die Stadt gebaut haben wollten. Zur Verteidigung schien ja der Ort nicht besonders geeignet, von der Natur geschützt war er nur gegenüber dem Fluß und gerade hier war ja der Schutz am wenigsten notwendig, eher wäre hier freie und leichte Ausfahrtmöglichkeit zu wünschen gewesen; von allen andern Seiten her war aber die Hochebene ohne Mühe zugänglich, deshalb also und auch wegen ihrer großen Ausdehnung schwer zu verteidigen. Außerdem war der Boden dort oben auf seine Ertragfähigkeit hin noch nicht untersucht, und vom Unterland abhängig bleiben und auf Fuhrwerkverkehr angewiesen sein, war für eine Stadt immer gefährlich, gar in unruhigen Zeiten. Auch ob genügendes Trinkwasser oben zu finden war, war noch nicht festgestellt, die kleine Quelle, die man mir zeigte, schien nicht zuverlässig. »Du bist müde«, sagte einer von ihnen, »du willst die Stadt nicht bauen.« »Müde bin ich«, sagte ich und setzte mich auf einen Stein neben die Quelle. Sie tauchten ein Tuch in das Wasser und erfrischten damit mein Gesicht, ich dankte ihnen. Dann sagte ich, daß ich einmal allein die Hochebene umgehen wolle und verließ sie; der Weg dauerte lang; als ich zurückkam, war es schon dunkel; alle lagen um die Quelle und schliefen; ein leichter Regen fiel.

Am Morgen wiederholte ich meine Frage; sie verstanden nicht gleich, wie ich die Frage des Abends am Morgen wiederholen könne. Dann aber sagten sie, sie könnten mir die Gründe, aus welchen

and soon they were at the top. I went up too and asked them why they wanted the city to be built precisely here. The place did not seem to be particularly suitable for purposes of defense, its only natural protection was on the riverside, and precisely there, after all, protection was least necessary; on the contrary, here was where one would have wished to have the means of setting out easily and freely; but the plateau was easily accessible from all other sides, and for that reason, and also because of its greater expanse, difficult to defend. Apart from this, the ground up there had not yet been tested for its fertility, and to remain dependent on the lowlands and at the mercy of transport was always a dangerous thing for a city, especially in times of unrest. Further, it had not yet been established whether there was enough drinking water available up there; the little spring they showed me did not seem good enough to rely on.

"You're tired," one of them said, "you don't want to build the city." "Yes, I'm tired," I said and sat down on a boulder near the spring. They dipped a cloth in the water and freshened my face with it. I thanked them. Then I said that I wanted to walk round the plateau once by myself, and left them; it took a long time; when I came back it was dark; they were all lying round the spring, asleep; a light rain was falling.

In the morning I repeated my question. They did not immediately understand how I could repeat the evening's question in the morning. Then, however, they said they could not give me the exact reasons for which they had chosen this place, but there were

sie diesen Ort gewählt hätten, nicht genau angeben, es seien alte Überlieferungen, welche diesen Ort empfehlen. Schon die Voreltern hätten die Stadt hier bauen wollen, aber aus irgenwelchen auch nicht genau überlieferten Gründen hätten sie doch nicht angefangen. Jedenfalls also sei es nicht Mutwille, der sie zu diesem Ort geführt habe, im Gegenteil, der Ort gefalle ihnen nicht einmal sehr und die Gegengründe, die ich angeführt habe, hätten sie auch selbst schon herausgefunden und als unwiderleglich anerkannt, aber es sei eben jene Überlieferung da, und wer der Überlieferung nicht folge, werde vernichtet. Deshalb sei ihnen unverständlich, warum ich zögere und nicht schon gestern zu bauen angefangen habe.

Ich beschloß fortzugehn und kletterte den Abhang zum Fluß hinab. Aber einer von ihnen war erwacht und hatte die andern geweckt und nun standen sie oben am Rand und ich war erst in der Mitte und sie baten und riefen mich. Da kehrte ich zurück, sie halfen mir und zogen mich hinauf. Ich verspach ihnen jetzt, die Stadt zu bauen. Sie waren sehr dankbar, hielten Reden an mich, küßten mich.

ancient traditions that recommended the place. Even their forefathers had wanted to build the city here, but for some reasons, which tradition did not record exactly either, they had not begun after all. In any case, then, it was no wanton whim that had led them to this place; on the contrary they did not even much care for the place, and the counterarguments I had brought forward they had already thought of for themselves and acknowledged to be irrefutable, but there it was, they said, there was this tradition, and anyone who did not follow tradition would be annihilated. For this reason, they said, they could not understand why I was hesitating and had not, indeed, begun to build the day before.

I resolved to go away, and climbed down the cliff to the river. But one of them had awakened and had waked the others and now they stood on the edge of the cliff and I was only halfway down and they pleaded and called to me. So I turned back, they helped me and pulled me up. I now promised them that I would build the city. They were very grateful, made speeches to me, kissed me.

Man schämt sich zu sagen, womit der kaiserliche Oberst unser Bergstädtchen beherrscht. Seine wenigen Soldaten wären, wenn wir wollten, gleich entwaffnet, Hilfe für ihn käme, selbst wenn er sie rufen könnte— aber wie könnte er das?—tage- ja wochenlang nicht. Er ist also völlig auf unsern Gehorsam angewiesen, sucht ihn aber weder durch Tyrannei zu erzwingen, noch durch Herzlichkeit zu erschmeicheln. Warum dulden wir also seine verhaßte Regierung? Es ist zweifellos: nur seines Blickes wegen. Wenn man in sein Arbeitszimmer kommt, vor einem Jahrhundert war es der Beratungssaal unserer Ältesten, sitzt er in Uniform an dem Schreibtisch, die Feder in der Hand. Förmlichkeiten oder gar Komödiespielen liebt er nicht, er schreibt also nicht etwa weiter und läßt den Besucher warten, sondern unterbricht die Arbeit sofort und lehnt sich zurück, die Feder allerdings behält er in der Hand. Nun sieht er zurückgelehnt, die Linke in der Hosentasche, den Besucher an. Der Bittsteller hat den Eindruck, daß der Oberst mehr sieht als nur ihn, den für ein Weilchen aus der Menge aufgetauchten Unbekannten, denn warum würde ihn denn der Oberst so genau und lange und stumm ansehn. Es ist auch kein scharfer prüfender, sich einbohrender Blick, wie man ihn vielleicht auf einen Einzelnen richten kann, sondern es ist ein nachlässiger, schweifender, allerdings aber unablässiger Blick, ein Blick, mit dem man etwa die Bewegungen

One is ashamed to say by what means the imperial colonel governs our little town in the mountains. His few soldiers could be disarmed immediately, if we so wished, and help for him, even supposing he could summon it—but how could he do that?—would not come for days, indeed for weeks. And so he is utterly dependent on our obedience, but he does not try either to enforce it by tyrannical means or to wheedle it out of us by cordiality. And so why do we tolerate his hated rule? There is no doubt about it: only because of his gaze. When one enters his study—a century ago it was the council chamber of our elders—there he sits at his desk, in uniform, pen in hand. Ceremonial is something he does not care for, and any form of play-acting far less, and so he does not go on writing, as he might, letting the visitor wait, but instantly interrupts his work and leans back, though he does keep his pen in his hand. And so, leaning back, his left hand in his trouser pocket, he gazes at the visitor. The petitioner has the impression that the colonel sees more than merely him, the unknown person who has emerged from the crowd for a little while, for why else should the colonel scrutinize him so closely, and long, and in silence? Nor is it a keen, probing, penetrating gaze, such as might be directed at an individual person; it is a nonchalant, roving, and yet steady gaze, a gaze with which one might, for instance, observe the movements of a crowd in the distance. And this

einer Menschenmenge in der Ferne beobachten würde.
Und dieser lange Blick ist ununterbrochen begleitet
von einem unbestimmten Lächeln, das bald Ironie,
bald träumendes Erinnern zu sein scheint.

DER KAISER

Ein Mann bezweifelte die göttliche Abstammung des
Kaisers, er behauptete, der Kaiser sei mit Recht unser
oberster Herr, bezweifelte nicht die göttliche Sendung
des Kaisers, die war ihm sichtbar, nur die göttliche
Abstammung bezweifelte er. Viel Aufsehen machte
das natürlich nicht; wenn die Brandung einen Was-
sertropfen ans Land wirft, stört das nicht den ewigen
Wellengang des Meeres, es ist vielmehr von ihm
bedingt.

long gaze is continuously accompanied by an inde-
finable smile, which seems to be now irony, now
dreamy reminiscence.

THE EMPEROR

A man doubted that the emperor was descended
from the gods; he asserted that the emperor was our
rightful sovereign, he did not doubt the emperor's
divine mission (that was evident to him), it was only
the divine descent that he doubted. This, naturally, did
not cause much of a stir; when the surf flings a drop
of water on to the land, that does not interfere with
the eternal rolling of the sea, on the contrary, it is
caused by it.

In der Karawanserei war niemals Schlaf, dort schlief
niemand; aber wenn man dort nicht schlief, warum
ging man hin? Um das Tragvieh ausruhn zu lassen.
Es war nur ein kleiner Ort, eine winzige Oase, aber
sie war ganz von der Karawanserei ausgefüllt und die
war nun allerdings riesenhaft. Es war für einen Fremden, so schien es mir wenigstens, unmöglich, sich dort
zurechtzufinden. Die Bauart verschuldete das auch.
Man kam zum Beispiel in den ersten Hof, aus dem
führten etwa zehn Meter voneinander entfernt zwei
Rundbögen in einen zweiten Hof, man ging durch
den einen Bogen und kam nun statt in einen neuen
großen Hof, wie man erwartet hatte, auf einen kleinen
finstern Platz zwischen himmelhohen Mauern, erst
weit in der Höhe sah man beleuchtete Loggien. Nun
glaubte man sich also geirrt zu haben und wollte in
den ersten Hof zurückgehn, man ging aber zufällig
nicht durch den Bogen zurück, durch den man gekom-
men war, sondern durch den zweiten nebenan. Aber
nun war man doch nicht auf dem ersten Platz,
sondern in einem andern viel größeren Hof voll
Lärm, Musik und Viehgebrüll. Man hatte sich also
geirrt, ging wieder auf den dunklen Platz zurück
und durch den ersten Türbogen. Es half nichts,
wieder war man auf dem zweiten Platz und man
mußte durch einige Höfe sich durchfragen, ehe man
wieder in den ersten Hof kam, den man doch eigentlich mit ein paar Schritten verlassen hatte. Unan-

In the caravansary there was never any sleep, there no one slept. But if one did not sleep there, why did one go at all? In order to let the beasts of burden rest. It was only a small place, a tiny oasis, but it was entirely occupied by the caravansary and that, to be sure, was immense. It was impossible, or at least so it seemed to me, for a stranger to find his way about there. The manner in which it was built was partly to blame for this. For instance, one went into the first courtyard, out of which two round arches, about thirty feet distant from each other, led into a second court; one went through one arch and then, instead of coming into another large court, as one had expected, found oneself in a small gloomy square between walls that were sky-high, and only at a great height above one did one see loggias with light burning. And so now one thought one had lost one's way and tried to go back through the archway, but, as it happened, one did not go through the archway one had come through but through the other one next to it. But now one was not in the first courtyard after all, but in another and much larger court, full of noise, music, and the bellowing of animals. So one had lost one's way, went back into the dark square and through the first arch. It was of no avail, once again one was in the second court and had to ask one's way through several courtyards before arriving back in the first courtyard, from which one had, however, actually gone

genehm war nun, daß der erste Hof immer überfüllt
war, dort konnte man kaum ein Unterkommen finden.
Es sah fast so aus, als ob die Wohnungen im ersten
Hof von ständigen Gästen besetzt seien, aber es
konnte doch in Wirklichkeit nicht sein, denn hier
wohnten nur Karawanen, wer hätte sonst in diesem
Schmutz und Lärm leben wollen oder können, die
kleine Oase gab ja nichts her als Wasser und war
viele Meilen von größeren Oasen entfernt. Also
ständig wohnen, leben wollen, konnte hier niemand,
es wäre denn der Besitzer der Karawanserei und seine
Angestellten, aber die habe ich, trotzdem ich einigemal
dort gewesen bin, nie gesehn, auch nichts von ihnen
gehört. Es wäre auch schwer vorzustellen gewesen,
daß, wenn ein Besitzer vorhanden war, er solche
Unordnung, ja Gewalttaten zugelassen hätte, wie sie
dort üblich waren bei Tag und Nacht. Ich hatte
vielmehr den Eindruck, daß die jeweilig stärkste
Karawane dort herrschte und dann, nach der Stärke
abgestuft, die andern. Allerdings alles wird dadurch
nicht erklärt. Das große Eingangstor zum Beispiel
war gewöhnlich fest verschlossen; es Karawanen zu
öffnen, die kamen oder gingen, war immer eine
geradezu feierliche Handlung, die man auf umständ-
liche Weise erwirken mußte. Oft standen Karawanen
draußen stundenlang im Sonnenbrand, ehe man sie
einließ. Das war zwar offene Willkür, aber man kam
ihr doch nicht auf den Grund. Man stand also
draußen und hatte Zeit, die Umrahmung des alten
Tores zu betrachten. Es waren rings um das Tor in
zwei, drei Reihen Engel in Hochrelief, die Fanfaren

only a few paces away. What was unpleasant, now, was that the first courtyard was always crowded, one could scarcely find any lodging there. It looked almost as though the quarters in the first courtyard were occupied by permanent guests, yet it could not be so in reality, for only caravans stopped here, who else would have wanted or been able to live in this dirt and uproar; after all, the little oasis provided nothing but water and was many miles away from larger oases. And so nobody could want to lodge, to live, here permanently, unless it was the owner of the caravansary and his employees, but these people I never saw, in spite of having been there several times, nor did I ever hear anything about them. And it would have been difficult to imagine that if an owner had been present he would have permitted such disorder, indeed such acts of violence, as were usual there by day and night. On the contrary, I had the impression that whichever happened to be the strongest caravan dominated everything there, and then came the others, according to their strength. True, that does not explain everything. The great main gate, for instance, was usually locked and barred; to open it for caravans coming or going was always a positively ceremonial act, and to bring this about was a very complicated matter. Caravans would often wait outside in the glaring sunshine for hours before they were let in. This, of course, was obviously wanton behavior, but one could never discover the reason for it. And so one waited outside and had time to contemplate the framework of the ancient gateway. Round the gate there

bliesen; eines dieser Instrumente, gerade auf der Höhe der Torwölbung, ragte tief genug in die Toreinfahrt hinab. Die Tiere mußten immer vorsichtig herumgeführt werden, daß sie nicht daran schlugen, es war merkwürdig, insbesondere bei der Verfallenheit des ganzen Baus, daß diese allerdings schöne Arbeit gar nicht beschädigt war, nicht einmal von denen, die solange in ohnmächtigen Zorn vor dem Tor schon gewartet hatten.

were two or three ranks of angels in high relief, blowing trumpets; one of these instruments, right at the apex of the arch, extended fairly far down into the gateway itself. The animals always had to be carefully led round it, so that they should not bump against it; it was strange, particularly in view of the ruinous condition of the whole building, that this work, beautiful as it was, was not damaged at all, not even by those who had been waiting so long in impotent anger outside the gate.

»Wie bin ich hierhergekommen?« rief ich. Es war ein
mäßig großer, von mildem elektrischem Licht be-
leuchteter Saal, dessen Wände ich abschritt. Es waren
zwar einige Türen vorhanden, öffnete man sie aber,
dann stand man vor einer dunklen glatten Felswand,
die kaum eine Handbreit von der Türschwelle entfernt war und geradlinig aufwärts und nach beiden
Seiten in unabsehbare Ferne verlief. Hier war kein
Ausweg. Nur eine Tür führte in ein Nebenzimmer,
die Aussicht dort war hoffnungsreicher, aber nicht
weniger befremdend als bei den andern Türen. Man
sah in ein Fürstenzimmer, Rot und Gold herrschte
dort vor, es gab dort mehrere wandhohe Speigel und
einen großen Glaslüster. Aber das war noch nicht
alles.

Ich muß nicht mehr zurück, die Zelle ist gesprengt,
ich bewege mich, ich fühle meinen Körper.

"How did I get here?" I exclaimed. It was a moderately large hall, lit by soft electric light, and I was walking along close to the walls. Although there were several doors, if one opened them one only found oneself standing in front of a dark, smooth rock-face, scarcely a handbreadth beyond the threshold and extending vertically upwards and horizontally on both sides, seemingly without any end. Here was no way out. Only one door led into an adjoining room, the prospect there was more hopeful, but no less startling than that behind the other doors. One looked into a royal apartment, the prevailing colors were red and gold, there were several mirrors as high as the ceiling, and a large glass chandelier. But that was not all.

I do not have to go back again, the cell is burst open, I move, I feel my body.

Wenn wir vom Teufel besessen sind, dann kann es
nicht einer sein, denn sonst lebten wir wenigstens auf
der Erde, ruhig, wie mit Gott, einheitlich, ohne Widerspruch, ohne Überlegung, unseres Hintermannes immer gewiss. Sein Gesicht würde uns nicht erschrecken,
denn als Teuflische wären wir bei einiger Empfind-
lichkeit für diesen Anblick klug genug, lieber eine
Hand zu opfern, mit der wir sein Gesicht bedeckt
hielten. Wenn uns nur ein einziger Teufel hätte, mit
ruhigem ungestörtem Überblick über unser ganzes
Wesen und mit augenblicklicher Verfügungsfreiheit,
dann hätte er auch genügende Kraft, uns ein mensch-
liches Leben lang so hoch über dem Geist Gottes in
uns zu halten und noch zu schwingen, dass wir auch
keinen Schimmer von ihm zu sehen bekämen, also
auch von dort nicht beunruhigt würden. Nur die
Menge der Teufel kann unser irdisches Unglück
ausmachen. Warum rotten sie einander nicht aus bis
auf einen oder warum unterordnen sie sich nicht einem
grossen Teufel? Beides wäre im Sinne des teuflischen
Prinzips, uns möglichst vollkommen zu betrügen. Was
nützt denn, so lange die Einheitlichkeit fehlt, die
peinliche Sorgfalt, die sämtliche Teufel für uns haben?
Es ist nur selbstverständlich, dass den Teufeln an dem
Ausfallen eines Menschenhaares mehr gelegen sein
muss als Gott, denn dem Teufel geht das Haar wirklich verloren, Gott nicht. Nur kommen wir dadurch,
solange die vielen Teufel in uns sind, noch immer zu
keinem Wohlbefinden.

THE INVENTION OF THE DEVIL

If we are possessed by the devil, it cannot be by one, for then we should live, at least here on earth, quietly, as with God, in unity, without contradiction, without reflection, always sure of the man behind us. His face would not frighten us, for as diabolical beings we would, if somewhat sensitive to the sight, be clever enough to prefer to sacrifice a hand in order to keep his face covered with it. If we were possessed by only a single devil, one who had a calm untroubled view of our whole nature, and freedom to dispose of us at any moment, then that devil would also have enough power to hold us for the length of a human life high above the spirit of God in us and even to swing us to and fro, so that we should never get to see a glimmer of it, and therefore should not be troubled from that quarter. Only a crowd of devils could account for our earthly misfortunes. Why don't they exterminate one another until only a single one is left, or why don't they subordinate themselves to one great devil? Either way would be in accord with the diabolical principle of deceiving us as completely as possible. With unity lacking, of what use is the scrupulous attention all the devils pay us? It simply goes without saying that the falling of a human hair must matter more to the devil than to God, since the devil really loses that hair and God does not. But as long as many devils are in us that still does not help us arrive at any state of well-being.

Jenen Wilden, von denen erzählt wird, daß sie kein
anderes Verlangen haben als zu sterben oder vielmehr
sie haben nicht einmal mehr dieses Verlangen, sondern der Tod hat nach ihnen Verlangen und sie geben
sich hin oder vielmehr sie geben sich nicht einmal
hin, sondern sie fallen in den Ufersand und stehn
niemals mehr auf—jenen Wilden gleiche ich sehr
und habe auch Stammesbrüder ringsherum, aber die
Verwirrung in diesen Ländern ist so groß, das Ge-
dränge wogt auf und ab bei Tag und Nacht und die
Brüder lassen sich von ihm tragen. Das nennt man
hierzulande, einem unter den Arm greifen‘, solche
Hilfe ist hier immer bereit; einen, der ohne Grund
umsinken könnte und liegenbliebe, fürchtet man wie
den Teufel, es ist wegen des Beispiels, es ist wegen
des Gestankes der Wahrheit, der aus ihm steigen
würde. Gewiß, es würde nichts geschehn, einer, zehn,
ein ganzes Volk könnte liegenbleiben und es würde
nichts geschehn, weiter ginge das mächtige Leben,
noch übervoll sind die Dachböden von Fahnen, die
niemals aufgerollt gewesen sind, dieser Leierkasten
hat nur eine Walze, aber die Ewigkeit in eigener
Person dreht die Kurbel. Und doch die Angst! Wie
tragen doch die Leute ihren eigenen Feind, so ohnmächtig er ist, immer in sich. Seinetwegen, dieses
ohnmächtigen Feindes wegen, sind sie . . .

Those savages of whom it is recounted that they have no other longing than to die, or rather, they no longer have even that longing, but death has a longing for them, and they abandon themselves to it, or rather, they do not even abandon themselves, but fall into the sand on the shore and never get up again—those savages I much resemble, and indeed I have fellow clansmen round about, but the confusion in these territories is so great, the tumult is like waves rising and falling by day and by night, and the brothers let themselves be borne upon it. That is what, in this country, is called "giving someone a leg up"; everyone here is always ready with such help. Anyone who might collapse without cause and remain lying on the ground is dreaded as though he were the Devil, it is because of the example, it is because of the stench of truth that would emanate from him. Granted, nothing would happen; one, ten, a whole nation might very well remain lying on the ground and nothing would happen; life in all its might would go on just the same; the attics are still chockablock with flags that were never unfurled; this barrel organ can play only one tune, but it is eternity in person that turns the handle. And yet the fear! How people do always carry their own enemy, however powerless he is, within themselves.

Zwei Knaben sassen auf der Quaimauer und spielten Würfel. Ein Mann las eine Zeitung auf den Stufen eines Denkmals im Schatten des säbelschwingenden Helden. Ein Mädchen am Brunnen füllte Wasser in ihre Bütte. Ein Obstverkäufer lag neben seiner Ware und blickte auf den See hinaus. In der Tiefe einer Kneipe sah man durch die leeren Tür-und Fensterlöcher zwei Männer beim Wein. Der Wirt sass vorn an einem Tisch und schlummerte. Eine Barke schwebte leise, als werde sie über dem Wasser getragen, in den kleinen Hafen. Ein Mann in blauem Kittel stieg ans Land und zog die Seile durch die Ringe. Zwei andere Männer in dunklen Röcken mit Silberknöpfen trugen hinter dem Bootsmann eine Bahre, auf der unter einem grossen blumengemusterten, gefransten Seidentuch offenbar ein Mensch lag.

Auf dem Quai kümmerte sich niemand um die Ankömmlinge, selbst als sie die Bahre niederstellten, um auf den Bootsführer zu warten, der noch an den Seilen arbeitete, trat niemand heran, niemand richtete eine Frage an sie, niemand sah sie genauer an.

Der Führer wurde noch ein wenig aufgehalten durch eine Frau, die, ein Kind an der Brust, mit aufgelösten Haaren sich jetzt auf Deck zeigte. Dann kam er, wies auf ein gelbliches, zweistöckiges Haus, das sich links nahe beim Wasser geradlinig erhob, die Träger nahmen die Last auf und trugen sie durch das niedrige, aber von schlanken Säulen gebildete Tor. Ein kleiner Junge

Two boys were sitting on the harbor wall playing with dice. A man was reading a newspaper on the steps of the monument, resting in the shadow of a hero who was flourishing his sword on high. A girl was filling her bucket at the fountain. A fruit-seller was lying beside his scales, staring out to sea. Through the vacant window and door openings of a café one could see two men quite at the back drinking their wine. The proprietor was sitting at a table in front and dozing. A bark was silently making for the little harbor, as if borne by invisible means over the water. A man in a blue blouse climbed ashore and drew the rope through a ring. Behind the boatman two other men in dark coats with silver buttons carried a bier, on which, beneath a great flower-patterned tasseled silk cloth, a man was apparently lying.

Nobody on the quay troubled about the newcomers; even when they lowered the bier to wait for the boatman, who was still occupied with his rope, nobody went nearer, nobody asked them a question, nobody accorded them an inquisitive glance.

The pilot was still further detained by a woman who, a child at her breast, now appeared with loosened hair on the deck of the boat. Then he advanced and indicated a yellowish two-storied house that rose abruptly on the left beside the sea; the bearers took up their burden and bore it to the low but gracefully pillared door. A little boy opened a window just in time to see

öffnete ein Fenster, bemerkte noch gerade, wie der Trupp im Haus verschwand, und schloss wieder eilig das Fenster. Auch das Tor wurde nun geschlossen, es war aus schwarzem Eichenholz sorgfältig gefügt. Ein Taubenschwarm, der bisher den Glockenturm umflogen hatte, liess sich jetzt vor dem Hause nieder. Als werde im Hause ihre Nahrung aufbewahrt, sammelten sich die Tauben vor dem Tor. Eine flog bis zum ersten Stock auf und pickte an die Fensterscheibe. Es waren hellfarbige, wohlgepflegte, lebhafte Tiere. In grossem Schwung warf ihnen die Frau aus der Barke Körner hin, die sammelten sie auf und flogen dann zu der Frau hinüber.

Ein Mann im Zylinderhut mit Trauerband kam eine der schmalen, stark abfallenden Gässchen, die zum Hafen führten, herab. Er blickte aufmerksam umher, alles bekümmerte ihn, der Anblick von Unrat in einem Winkel liess ihn das Gesicht verzerren. Auf den Stufen des Denkmals lagen Obstschalen, er schob sie im Vorbeigehen mit seinem Stock hinunter. An der Stubentür klopfte er an, gleichzeitig nahm er den Zylinderhut in seine schwarzbehandschuhte Rechte. Gleich wurde geöffnet, wohl fünfzig kleine Knaben bildeten ein Spalier im langen Flurgang und verbeugten sich.

Der Bootsführer kam die Treppe herab, begrüsste den Herrn, führte ihn hinauf, im ersten Stockwerk umging er mit ihm den von leicht gebauten, zierlichen Loggien umgebenen Hof und beide traten, während die Knaben in respektvoller Entfernung nachdrängten, in einen kühlen, grossen Raum an der Hinterseite des Hauses, dem gegenüber kein Haus mehr, sondern nur

the party vanishing into the house, then hastily shut the window again. The door too was now shut; it was of black oak, and very strongly made. A flock of doves which had been flying round the belfry alighted in the street before the house. As if their food were stored within, they assembled in front of the door. One of them flew up to the first story and pecked at the windowpane. They were bright-hued, well-tended, beautiful birds. The woman on the boat flung grain to them in a wide sweep; they ate it up and flew across to the woman.

A man in a top hat tied with a band of crêpe now descended one of the narrow and very steep lanes that led to the harbor. He glanced round vigilantly, everything seemed to displease him, his mouth twisted at the sight of some offal in a corner. Fruit skins were lying on the steps of the monument; he swept them off in passing with his stick. He rapped at the house door, at the same time taking his top hat from his head with his black-gloved hand. The door was opened at once, and some fifty little boys appeared in two rows in the long entry-hall, and bowed to him.

The boatman descended the stairs, greeted the gentleman in black, conducted him up to the first story, led him round the bright and elegant loggia which encircled the courtyard, and both of them entered, while the boys pressed after them at a respectful distance, a cool spacious room looking towards the back, from whose window no habitation, but only a bare, blackish-gray rocky wall was to be seen. The bearers were busied in setting up and lighting several long candles at the head

eine kahle, grau-schwarze Felsenwand zu sehen war. Die Träger waren damit beschäftigt, zu Häupten der Bahre einige lange Kerzen aufzustellen und anzuzünden, aber Licht entstand dadurch nicht, es wurden förmlich nur die früher ruhenden Schatten aufgescheucht und flackerten über die Wände. Von der Bahre war das Tuch zurückgeschlagen. Es lag dort ein Mann mit wild durcheinandergewachsenem Haar und Bart, gebräunter Haut, etwa einem Jäger gleichend. Er lag bewegungslos, scheinbar atemlos mit geschlossenen Augen da, trotzdem deutete nur die Umgebung an, dass es vielleicht ein Toter war.

Der Herr trat zur Bahre, legte eine Hand dem Daliegenden auf die Stirn, kniete dann nieder und betete. Der Bootsführer winkte den Trägern, das Zimmer zu verlassen, sie gingen hinaus, vertrieben die Knaben, die sich draussen angesammelt hatten, und schlossen die Tür. Dem Herrn schien aber auch diese Stille noch nicht zu genügen, er sah den Bootsführer an, dieser verstand und ging durch eine Seitentür ins Nebenzimmer. Sofort schlug der Mann auf der Bahre die Augen auf, wandte schmerzlich lächelnd das Gesicht dem Herrn zu und sagte: "Wer bist Du?" Der Herr erhob sich ohne weiteres Staunen aus seiner knieenden Stellung und antwortete: "Der Bürgermeister von Riva."

Der Mann auf der Bahre nickte, zeigte mit schwach ausgestrecktem Arm auf einen Sessel und sagte, nachdem der Bürgermeister seiner Einladung gefolgt war: "Ich wusste es ja, Herr Bürgermeister, aber im ersten Augenblick habe ich immer alles vergessen, alles geht

of the bier, yet these did not give light, but only scared away the shadows which had been immobile till then, and made them flicker over the walls. The cloth covering the bier had been thrown back. Lying on it was a man with wildly matted hair, who looked somewhat like a hunter. He lay without motion and, it seemed, without breathing, his eyes closed; yet only his trappings indicated that this man was probably dead.

The gentleman stepped up to the bier, laid his hand on the brow of the man lying upon it, then kneeled down and prayed. The boatman made a sign to the bearers to leave the room; they went out, drove away the boys who had gathered outside, and shut the door. But even that did not seem to satisfy the gentleman, he glanced at the boatman; the boatman understood, and vanished through a side door into the next room. At once the man on the bier opened his eyes, turned his face painfully towards the gentleman, and said: "Who are you?" Without any mark of surprise the gentleman rose from his kneeling posture and answered: "The Burgomaster of Riva."

The man on the bier nodded, indicated a chair with a feeble movement of his arm, and said, after the Burgomaster had accepted his invitation: "I knew that, of course, Burgomaster, but in the first moments of returning consciousness I always forget, everything goes round before my eyes, and it is best to ask about anything even if I know. You too probably know that I am the hunter Gracchus."

"Certainly," said the Burgomaster. "Your arrival was announced to me during the night. We had been asleep

mir in der Runde, und es ist besser, ich frage, auch wenn ich alles weiss. Auch Sie wissen wahrscheinlich, dass ich der Jäger Gracchus bin."

"Gewiss," sagte der Bürgermeister. "Sie wurden mir heute in der Nacht angekündigt. Wir schliefen längst. Da rief gegen Mitternacht meine Frau: 'Salvatore,'—so heisse ich—'sieh die Taube am Fenster!' Es war wirklich eine Taube, aber gross wie ein Hahn. Sie flog zu meinem Ohr und sagte: 'Morgen kommt der tote Jäger Gracchus, empfange ihn im Namen der Stadt.'"

Der Jäger nickte und zog die Zungenspitze zwischen den Lippen durch: "Ja, die Tauben fliegen vor mir her. Glauben Sie aber, Herr Bürgermeister, das ich in Riva bleiben soll?"

"Das kann ich noch nicht sagen," antwortete der Bürgermeister. "Sind Sie tot?"

"Ja," sagte der Jäger, "wie Sie sehen. Vor vielen Jahren, es müssen aber ungemein viel Jahre sein, stürzte ich im Schwarzwald—das ist in Deutschland—von einem Felsen, als ich eine Gemse verfolgte. Seitdem bin ich tot."

"Aber Sie leben doch auch," sagte der Bürgermeister.

"Gewissermassen," sagte der Jäger, "gewissermassen lebe ich auch. Mein Todeskahn verfehlte die Fahrt, eine falsche Drehung des Steuers, ein Augenblick der Unaufmerksamkeit des Führers, eine Ablenkung durch meine wunderschöne Heimat, ich weiss nicht, was es war, nur das weiss ich, dass ich auf der Erde blieb, und dass mein Kahn seither die irdischen Gewässer befährt. So reise ich, der nur in seinen Bergen leben

for a good while. Then towards midnight my wife cried: 'Salvatore'—that's my name—'look at that dove at the window.' It was really a dove, but as big as a cock. It flew over me and said in my ear: 'Tomorrow the dead hunter Gracchus is coming; receive him in the name of the city.'"

The hunter nodded and licked his lips with the tip of his tongue: "Yes, the doves flew here before me. But do you believe, Burgomaster, that I shall remain in Riva?"

"I cannot say that yet," replied the Burgomaster. "Are you dead?"

"Yes," said the hunter, "as you see. Many years ago, yes, it must be a great many years ago, I fell from a precipice in the Black Forest—that is in Germany—when I was hunting a chamois. Since then I have been dead."

"But you are alive too," said the Burgomaster.

"In a certain sense," said the hunter, "in a certain sense I am alive too. My death ship lost its way; a wrong turn of the wheel, a moment's absence of mind on the pilot's part, a longing to turn aside towards my lovely native country, I cannot tell what it was; I only know this, that I remained on earth and that ever since my ship has sailed earthly waters. So I, who asked for nothing better than to live among my mountains, travel after my death through all the lands of the earth."

"And you have no part in the other world?" asked the Burgomaster, knitting his brow.

"I am for ever," replied the hunter, "on the great stair that leads up to it. On that infinitely wide and

wollte, nach meinem Tode durch alle Länder der Erde."

"Und Sie haben keinen Teil am Jenseits?" fragte der Bürgermeister mit gerunzelter Stirne.

"Ich bin," antwortete der Jäger, "immer auf der grossen Treppe, die hinaufführt. Auf dieser unendlich weiten Freitreppe treibe ich mich herum, bald oben, bald unten, bald rechts, bald links, immer in Bewegung. Aus dem Jäger ist ein Schmetterling geworden. Lachen Sie nicht."

"Ich lache nicht," verwahrte sich der Bürgermeister.

"Sehr einsichtig," sagte der Jäger. "Immer bin ich in Bewegung. Nehme ich aber den grössten Aufschwung und leuchtet mir schon oben das Tor, erwache ich auf meinem alten, in irgendeinem irdischen Gewässer öde steckenden Kahn. Der Grundfehler meines einstmaligen Sterbens umgrinst mich in meiner Kajüte. Julia, die Frau des Bootsführers, klopft und bringt mir zu meiner Bahre das Morgengetränk des Landes, dessen Küste wir gerade befahren. Ich liege auf einer Holzpritsche, habe—es ist kein Vergnügen, mich zu betrachten—ein schmutziges Totenhemd an, Haar und Bart, grau und schwarz, geht unentwirrbar durcheinander, meine Beine sind mit einem grossen, seidenen blumengemusterten, langgefransten Frauentuch bedeckt. Zu meinen Häupten steht eine Kirchenkerze und leuchtet mir. An der Wand mir gegenüber ist ein kleines Bild, ein Buschmann offenbar, der mit einem Speer nach mir zielt und hinter einem grossartig bemalten Schild sich möglichst deckt. Man begegnet auf Schiffen manchen dummen Darstellungen, die—

spacious stair I clamber about, sometimes up, sometimes down, sometimes on the right, sometimes on the left, always in motion. The hunter has been turned into a butterfly. Do not laugh."

"I am not laughing," said the Burgomaster in self-defense.

"That is very good of you," said the hunter. "I am always in motion. But when I make a supreme flight and see the gate actually shining before me, I awaken presently on my old ship, still stranded forlornly in some earthly sea or other. The fundamental error of my onetime death grins at me as I lie in my cabin. Julia, the wife of the pilot, knocks at the door and brings me on my bier the morning drink of the land whose coasts we chance to be passing. I lie on a wooden pallet, I wear—it cannot be a pleasure to look at me— a filthy winding sheet, my hair and beard, black tinged with gray, have grown together inextricably, my limbs are covered with a great flower-patterned woman's shawl with long fringes. A sacramental candle stands at my head and lights me. On the wall opposite me is a little picture, evidently of a Bushman who is aiming his spear at me and taking cover as best he can behind a beautifully painted shield. On shipboard one is often a prey to stupid imaginations, but that is the stupidest of them all. Otherwise my wooden case is quite empty. Through a hole in the side wall come in the warm airs of the southern night, and I hear the water slapping against the old boat.

"I have lain here ever since the time when, as the hunter Gracchus living in the Black Forest, I followed

se ist aber eine der dümmsten. Sonst ist mein Holzkäfig
ganz leer. Durch eine Luke der Seitenwand kommt die
warme Luft der südlichen Nacht, und ich höre das
Wasser an die alte Barke schlagen.

"Hier liege ich seit damals, als ich, noch lebendiger
Jäger Gracchus, zu Hause im Schwarzwald eine
Gemse verfolgte und abstürzte. Alles ging der Ordnung
nach. Ich verfolgte, stürzte ab, verblutete in einer
Schlucht, war tot, und diese Barke sollte mich ins
Jenseits tragen. Ich erinnere mich noch, wie fröhlich
ich mich hier auf der Pritsche ausstreckte zum ersten
Mal. Niemals haben die Berge solchen Gesang von mir
gehört wie diese vier damals noch dämmerigen Wände.

"Ich hatte gern gelebt und war gern gestorben,
glücklich warf ich, ehe ich den Bord betrat, das Lum-
penpack der Büchse, der Tasche, des Jagdgewehrs von
mir hinunter, das ich immer stolz getragen hatte, und
in das Totenhemd schlüpfte ich wie ein Mädchen ins
Hochzeitskleid. Hier lag ich und wartete. Dann
geschah das Unglück."

"Ein schlimmes Schicksal," sagte der Bürgermeister
mit abwehrend erhobener Hand. "Und Sie tragen gar
keine Schuld daran?"

"Keine," sagte der Jäger, "ich war Jäger, ist das etwa
eine Schuld? Aufgestellt war ich als Jäger im Schwarzwald, wo es damals noch Wölfe gab. Ich lauerte auf,
schoss, traf, zog das Fell ab, ist das eine Schuld? Meine
Arbeit wurde gesegnet. 'Der grosse Jäger vom Schwarzwald' hiess ich. Ist das eine Schuld?"

"Ich bin nicht berufen, das zu entscheiden," sagte
der Bürgermeister, "doch scheint auch mir keine

a chamois and fell from a precipice. Everything happened in good order. I pursued, I fell, bled to death in a ravine, died, and this ship should have conveyed me to the next world. I can still remember how gladly I stretched myself out on this pallet for the first time. Never did the mountains listen to such songs from me as these shadowy walls did then.

"I had been glad to live and I was glad to die. Before I stepped aboard, I joyfully flung away my wretched load of ammunition, my knapsack, my hunting rifle that I had always been proud to carry, and I slipped into my winding sheet like a girl into her marriage dress. I lay and waited. Then came the mishap."

"A terrible fate," said the Burgomaster, raising his hand defensively. "And you bear no blame for it?"

"None," said the hunter. "I was a hunter; was there any sin in that? I followed my calling as a hunter in the Black Forest, where there were still wolves in those days. I lay in ambush, shot, hit my mark, flayed the skins from my victims: was there any sin in that? My labors were blessed. 'The great hunter of the Black Forest' was the name I was given. Was there any sin in that?"

"I am not called upon to decide that," said the Burgomaster, "but to me also there seems to be no sin in such things. But, then whose is the guilt?"

"The boatman's," said the hunter. "Nobody will read what I say here, no one will come to help me; even if all the people were commanded to help me, every door and window would remain shut, everybody would take to bed and draw the bedclothes over his head, the

Schuld darin zu liegen. Aber wer trägt denn die Schuld?"

"Der Bootsmann," sagte der Jäger. "Niemand wird lesen, was ich hier schreibe, niemand wird kommen, mir zu helfen; wäre als Aufgabe gesetzt, mir zu helfen, so blieben alle Türen aller Häuser geschlossen, alle Fenster geschlossen, alle liegen in den Betten, die Decken über den Kopf geschlagen, eine nächtliche Herberge die ganze Erde. Das hat guten Sinn, denn niemand weiss von mir, und wüsste er von mir, so wüsste er meinen Aufenthalt nicht, und wüsste er meinen Aufenthalt, so wüsste er mich dort nicht festzuhalten, so wüsste er nicht, wie mir zu helfen. Der Gedanke, mir helfen zu wollen, ist eine Krankheit und muss im Bett geheilt werden.

"Das weiss ich und schreie also nicht, um Hilfe herbeizurufen, selbst wenn ich in Augenblicken—unbeherrscht wie ich bin, zum Beispiel gerade jetzt—sehr stark daran denke. Aber es genügt wohl zum Austreiben solcher Gedanken, wenn ich umherblicke und mir vergegenwärtige, wo ich bin und—das darf ich wohl behaupten—seit Jahrhunderten wohne."

"Ausserordentlich," sagte der Bürgermeister, "ausserordentlich.—Und nun gedenken Sie bei uns in Riva zu bleiben?"

"Ich gedenke nicht," sagte der Jäger lächelnd und legte, um den Spott gutzumachen, die Hand auf das Knie des Bürgermeisters. "Ich bin hier, mehr weiss ich nicht, mehr kann ich nicht tun. Mein Kahn ist ohne Steuer, er fährt mit dem Wind, der in den untersten Regionen des Todes bläst."

whole earth would become an inn for the night. And there is sense in that, for nobody knows of me, and if anyone knew he would not know where I could be found, and if he knew where I could be found, he would not know how to deal with me, he would not know how to help me. The thought of helping me is an illness that has to be cured by taking to one's bed.

"I know that, and so I do not shout to summon help, even though at moments—when I lose control over myself, as I have done just now, for instance—I think seriously of it. But to drive out such thoughts I need only look round me and verify where I am, and—I can safely assert—have been for hundreds of years."

"Extraordinary," said the Burgomaster, "extraordinary.—And now do you think of staying here in Riva with us?"

"I think not," said the hunter with a smile, and, to excuse himself, he laid his hand on the Burgomaster's knee. "I am here, more than that I do not know, further than that I cannot go. My ship has no rudder, and it is driven by the wind that blows in the undermost regions of death."

EIN FRAGMENT

"Wie ist es, Jäger Gracchus, du fährst schon seit Jahrhunderten in diesem alten Kahn?"

"Schon fünfzehnhundert Jahre."

"Und immer in diesem Schiff?"

"Immer in dieser Barke. Barke ist, meine ich, die richtige Bezeichnung. Du kennst dich im Schiffswesen nicht aus?"

"Nein, erst seit heute kümmere ich mich darum, seitdem ich von dir weiss, seitdem ich dein Schiff betreten habe."

"Keine Entschuldigung. Ich bin ja auch aus dem Binnenland. War kein Seefahrer, wollte es nicht werden, Berg und Wald waren meine Freunde, und jetzt—ältester Seefahrer, Jäger Gracchus, Schutzgeist der Matrosen, Jäger Gracchus, angebetet mit gerungenen Händen vom Schiffsjungen, der sich im Mastkorb ängstigt in der Sturmnacht. Lache nicht."

"Lachen sollte ich? Nein, wahrhaftig nicht. Mit Herzklopfen stand ich vor der Tür deiner Kajüte, mit Herzklopfen bin ich eingetreten. Dein freundliches Wesen beruhigt mich ein wenig, aber niemals werde ich vergessen, wessen Gast ich bin."

"Gewiss, du hast recht. Wie es auch sein mag, Jäger Gracchus bin ich. Willst du nicht von dem Wein trinken, die Marke kenne ich nicht, aber er ist süss und schwer, der Patron versorgt mich gut."

136

"What, Hunter Gracchus, have you been sailing in this old boat for centuries?"

"Fifteen hundred years by now."

"And always in this same ship?"

"In this same bark. Bark, I believe, is the right word. You're not familiar with nautical matters, are you?"

"No. Today's the first time I've ever taken any interest in them—only since I know about you, since I boarded your ship."

"No apologies necessary. I come from inland too. I was no seafarer, and never wanted to be one. The mountains and woods used to be my friends, and now: —oldest of seafarers, Hunter Gracchus, patron deity of sailors, Hunter Gracchus, to whom cabin boys pray, wringing their hands, when frightened in crow's nests on stormy nights. Don't laugh."

"Why should I laugh? No, not at all. I stood at the door of your cabin with beating heart, and with beating heart I entered it. Your friendly manner makes me feel a little calmer, but I shall never forget whose guest I am."

"You're right, of course. Come what may, I'm Hunter Gracchus. Don't you want to taste some of this wine? I don't know the brand, but it's sweet and heavy—the boss takes good care of me."

"Not just now, thanks, I feel too restless. Maybe

"Jetzt bitte nicht, ich bin zu unruhig. Vielleicht später, wenn du mich solange hier duldest. Auch wage ich es nicht, aus deinem Glas zu trinken. Wer ist der Patron?"

"Der Besitzer der Barke. Diese Patrone sind nämlich ausgezeichnete Menschen. Ich verstehe sie nur nicht. Ich meine nicht ihre Sprache, wiewohl ich natürlich auch ihre Sprache oft nicht verstehe. Aber dies nur nebenbei. Sprachen habe ich im Laufe der Jahrhunderte genug gelernt und könnte Dolmetscher sein zwischen den Vorfahren und den Heutigen. Aber den Gedankengang der Patrone verstehe ich nicht. Vielleicht kannst du es mir erklären."

"Viel Hoffnung habe ich nicht. Wie sollte ich dir etwas erklären können, da ich doch dir gegenüber kaum ein lallendes Kind bin."

"Nicht so, ein für allemal nicht. Du wirst mir einen Gefallen tun, wenn du etwas männlicher, etwas selbstbewusster auftrittst. Was fange ich an mit einem Schatten als Gast. Ich blase ihn aus der Luke auf den See hinaus. Ich brauche verschiedene Erklärungen. Du, der du dich draussen herumtreibst, kannst sie mir geben. Schlotterst du aber hier an meinem Tisch und vergisst durch Selbsttäuschung das Wenige, was du weisst, dann kannst du dich gleich packen. Wie ichs meine, so sag ichs."

"Es ist etwas Richtiges darin. Tatsächlich bin ich dir in manchem über. Ich werde mich also zu bezwingen suchen. Frage!"

"Besser, viel besser du übertreibst in dieser Richtung und bildest dir irgendwelche Überlegenheiten ein. Du

138

later, if you allow me to stay that long. Besides, I don't dare drink out of your glass. Who is the boss?"

"The owner of the bark. These bosses are certainly remarkable people. Only I don't understand them. I don't mean their language—although, of course, I often don't understand their language either. But that's beside the point—I've learned enough languages in the course of the centuries and could act as an interpreter between the present generation and its ancestors. But what I don't understand is the thought processes of the bosses. Perhaps you can explain them to me."

"I'm not very hopeful of that. How can I explain anything to you, when I'm not even a babbling infant in comparison?"

"That's not so, once and for all that's not so. You would be doing me a favor if you spoke up with a little more manliness, with a little more self-assurance. What good is it having a shadow for a guest? I'd blow him through the hatchway into the lake. I'm in need of a variety of explanations. You, who run around outside, can give them to me. But if you want to tremble here at my table and deceive yourself into forgetting what little you do know, why, you can get out immediately. I mean exactly what I say."

"There's something in what you say. Really, I am superior to you in many ways. So I'll try to control myself. Ask on!"

"That's better, much better. Now you're straining too far in the opposite direction and imagining that you're superior in some sorts of ways. But you must understand me correctly. I'm a human being like you, only

musst mich nur richtig verstehen. Ich bin Mensch wie du, aber um die paar Jahrhunderte ungeduldiger, um die ich älter bin. Also von den Patronen wollen wir sprechen. Gib acht! Und trinke Wein, damit du dir den Verstand schärfst. Ohne Scheu. Kräftig. Es ist noch eine grosse Schiffsladung da."

"Gracchus, das ist ein exzellenter Wein. Der Patron soll leben."

"Schade, dass er· heute gestorben ist. Er war ein guter Mann, und er ist friedlich hingegangen. Wohlgeratene erwachsene Kinder standen an seinem Sterbebett, am Fussende ist die Frau ohnmächtig hingefallen, sein letzter Gedanke aber galt mir. Ein guter Mann, ein Hamburger."

"Du lieber Himmel, ein Hamburger, und du weisst hier im Süden, dass er heute gestorben ist?"

"Wie? Ich sollte nicht wissen, wann mein Patron stirbt. Du bist doch recht einfältig."

"Willst du mich beleidigen?"

"Nein, gar nicht, ich tue es wider Willen. Aber du sollst nicht soviel staunen und mehr Wein trinken. Mit den Patronen aber verhält es sich folgendermassen: Die Barke hat doch ursprünglich keinem Menschen gehört."

"Gracchus, eine Bitte. Sag es mir zuerst kurz, aber zusammenhängend, wie es mit dir steht. Um die Wahrheit zu gestehen: ich weiss es nämlich nicht. Für dich sind es natürlich selbstverständliche Dinge, und du setzest, wie es deine Art ist, ihre Kenntnis bei der ganzen Welt voraus. Nun hat man aber in dem kurzen Menschenleben—das Leben ist nämlich kurz, Grac-

more impatient by the few centuries by which I'm older. So let us talk about bosses. Pay attention! Drink some wine to sharpen your wits. Don't be timid. Drink up. There's a big cargo of it still left."

"This wine is excellent, Gracchus. May your boss be happy."

"A pity that he died today. He was a good man, and he went peacefully. His healthy, grown children stood around his deathbed, his wife lay fainting at its foot; his last thought, however, was for me. A good man, a Hamburger."

"Good God, a Hamburger, and here in the South you know that he died today?"

"What? Why shouldn't I know it when my boss dies? But really, you are quite simple-minded."

"Are you trying to insult me?"

"No, not at all, I'm doing so against my will. But you shouldn't be so amazed and you should drink more wine. As for bosses, the situation is as follows: Originally the bark belonged to no one."

"Gracchus, a request. First tell me briefly but coherently how things are with you. To tell the truth, I actually don't know. Naturally, you take it all for granted and assume, as is your habit, that the whole world knows everything. But in this short human life of ours—life really is short, Gracchus, try to conceive of that for yourself—one has one's hands full trying to make something of oneself and one's family. As interesting as Gracchus the Hunter is—and that's conviction on my part, not servile flattery—one has no time to think about him, to find out about him, not to men-

chus, suche dir das begreiflich zu machen—, in diesem kurzen Leben hat man also alle Hände voll zu tun, um sich und seine Familie hochzubringen. So interessant nun der Jäger Gracchus ist—das ist Überzeugung, nicht Kriecherei—, man hat keine Zeit an ihn zu denken, sich nach ihm zu erkundigen oder sich gar Sorgen über ihn zu machen. Vielleicht auf dem Sterbebett, wie dein Hamburger, das weiss ich nicht. Dort hat vielleicht der fleissige **Mann** zum ersten Mal Zeit, sich auszustrecken, und durch die müssiggängerischen Gedanken streicht dann einmal der grüne Jäger Gracchus. Sonst aber, wie gesagt: ich wusste nichts von dir, Geschäfte halber bin ich hier im Hafen, sah die Barke, das Laufbrett lag bereit, ich ging hinüber—, aber nun wüsste ich gerne etwas im Zusammenhang über dich."

"Ach, im Zusammenhang. Die alten, alten Geschichten. Alle Bücher sind voll davon, in allen Schulen malen es die Lehrer an die Tafel, die Mutter träumt davon, während das Kind an der Brust trinkt, es ist das Geflüster in den Umarmungen, die Händler sagen es den Käufern, die Käufer den Händlern, die Soldaten singen es beim Marsch, der Prediger ruft es in die Kirche, Geschichtsschreiber sehen in ihrer Stube mit offenem Mund das längst Geschehene und beschreiben es unaufhörlich, in der Zeitung ist es gedruckt, und das Volk reicht es sich von Hand zu Hand, der Telegraph wurde erfunden, damit es schneller die Erde umkreist, man gräbt es in verschütteten Städten aus, und der Aufzug rast damit zum Dach der Wolkenkratzer. Die Passagiere der Eisenbahnen verkünden es

tion going to any trouble about him. Perhaps on the deathbed, like your Hamburger—but I don't know. There perhaps a busy man has his first chance to take time to stretch out, and then Gracchus the green hunter may at last stray into his idle thoughts. But otherwise, it's the way I've said. I knew nothing about you. Business brought me here to the harbor, I saw the bark, the gang-plank was down, I crossed it—. But now I'd like very much to know something coherent about you."

"Ah, coherent. The old, old stories. All the books are full of it; teachers draw it on the blackboards in every school; mothers dream about it while babies drink at their breasts; it's whispered in embraces; merchants tell it to their customers, their customers tell it to merchants; soldiers sing it on the march; preachers shout it in church; in their studies historians see with open mouths that which happened long ago, and describe it unceasingly; it's printed in newspapers and people pass it from hand to hand; the telegraph was invented so that it could circle the earth faster; it's excavated from buried cities, and elevators speed to the tops of skyscrapers with it. Railroad passengers announce it from train windows to the regions they travel through, but previously savages howled it at them; it can be read in the stars, and lakes carry its reflection; brooks bring it from the mountains, and you sit here, man, and ask me for coherence. You must have spent an exceptionally wasteful youth."

"Possibly, as is characteristic of all youth. But it would be very useful to you, I believe, if you once looked around in the world a bit. As peculiar as it may

aus den Fenstern in den Ländern, die sie durchfahren, aber früher noch heulen es ihnen die Wilden entgegen, in den Sternen ist es zu lesen, und die Seen tragen das Spiegelbild, die Bäche bringen es aus dem Gebirge, und du Mann sitzest hier und fragst mich nach dem Zusammenhang. Du musst eine auserlesen verluderte Jugend gehabt haben."

"Möglich, wie das jeder Jugend eigentümlich ist. Dir aber wäre es, glaube ich, sehr nützlich, wenn du dich einmal in der Welt ein wenig umsehen würdest. So komisch es dir scheinen mag, hier wundere ich mich fast selbst darüber, aber es ist doch so, du bist nicht der Gegenstand des Stadtgesprächs, von wie vielen Dingen man auch spricht, du bist nicht darunter, die Welt geht ihren Gang und du machst deine Fahrt, aber niemals bis heute habe ich bemerkt, dass ihr euch gekreuzt hättet."

"Das sind deine Beobachtungen, mein Lieber, andere haben andere Beobachtungen gemacht. Es gibt hier nur zwei Möglichkeiten. Entweder verschweigst du, was du von mir weisst, und hast irgendeine bestimmte Absicht dabei. Für diesen Fall sage ich dir ganz frei: du bist auf einem Abweg. Oder aber: du glaubst dich tatsächlich nicht an mich erinnern zu können, weil du meine Geschichte mit einer andern verwechselst. Für diesen Fall sage ich dir nur: Ich bin—nein, ich kann nicht, jeder weiss es, und gerade ich soll es dir erzählen! Es ist so lange her. Frage die Geschichtsschreiber! Sie sehen in ihrer Stube mit offenem Mund das längst Geschehene und beschreiben es unaufhörlich. Gehe zu ihnen und komm dann wieder. Es ist so lange her.

seem to you—and sitting here, I almost marvel at it myself—nevertheless it's true that you are not the subject of talk in the cities; no matter how many things get talked about, you're not among them. The world goes its way and you make your journeys, but not until today did I ever notice that they crossed each other."

"My dear fellow, that's what *you* have noticed. Other people have noticed other things. At this point there are only two possibilities. Either you are keeping quiet about what you know about me and in doing that have some definite purpose in mind. In that case I can tell you quite frankly: you're on the wrong track. Or else you really believe that you can't remember anything about me because you've confused my story with someone else's. In that case all I can tell you is: I am—no, I can't, everybody knows it, and why should I be the one to tell you! It was all so long ago. Ask the historians! In their studies they see with open mouths that which happened long ago, and describe it unceasingly. Go to them and then come back. It was all so long ago. How can I be expected to keep it all inside this overcrowded brain?"

"Wait, Gracchus, I'll make it easier for you. I'll ask you questions. Where did you come from?"

"From the Black Forest, as is universally known."

"Naturally, from the Black Forest. And you did some hunting there in the fourth century?"

"Man, do you know the Black Forest?"

"No."

"Really, you don't know anything. The helmsman's little child knows as much as you, probably much more.

Wie soll ich denn das in diesem übervollen Gehirn bewahren."

"Warte, Gracchus, ich werde es dir erleichtern, ich werde dich fragen. Woher stammst du?"

"Aus dem Schwarzwald, wie allbekannt."

"Natürlich aus dem Schwarzwald. Und dort hast du also im vierten Jahrhundert etwa gejagt?"

"Mensch, kennst du den Schwarzwald?"

"Nein."

"Du kennst wirklich gar nichts. Das kleine Kind des Steuermanns weiss mehr als du, wahrscheinlich viel mehr. Wer nur hat dich hereingetrieben? Es ist ein Verhängnis. Deine aufdringliche Bescheidenheit war tatsächlich nur allzu gut begründet. Ein Nichts bist du, das ich mit Wein anfülle. Nun kennst du also nicht einmal den Schwarzwald. Und ich bin dort geboren. Bis zum fünfundzwanzigsten Jahr habe ich dort gejagt. Hätte mich nicht die Gemse verlockt—so, nun weisst du es—, hätte ich ein langes, schönes Jägerleben gehabt, aber die Gemse lockte mich, ich stürzte ab und schlug mich auf Steinen tot. Frag nicht weiter. Hier bin ich, tot, tot, tot. Weiss nicht, warum ich hier bin. Wurde damals aufgeladen auf den Todeskahn, wie es sich gebührt, ein armseliger Toter, die drei, vier Hantierungen wurden mit mir gemacht, wie mit jedem, warum Ausnahmen machen mit dem Jäger Gracchus, alles war in Ordnung, ausgestreckt lag ich im Kahn."

Who on earth sent you here? It was fate. Actually, your obtrusive modesty was only too well justified. You are a nullity that I am filling up with wine. So you don't even know the Black Forest. And I was born there. Until my twenty-fifth year I hunted there. Had the chamois not led me on—so now you know it—I would have had a long and beautiful hunter's life. But the chamois led me on, I fell and was killed on the rocks. Do not ask any more. Here I am, dead, dead, dead. I don't know why I'm here. At that time I was laid on board the ferry of death, as was fitting for a dead man. The three or four businesses were done about me, as with everybody else—why make an exception of the Hunter Gracchus? Everything was in order, outstretched I lay in the boat."

Es war ein Geier, der hackte in meine Füße. Stiefel und Strümpfe hatte er schon aufgerissen, nun hackte er schon in die Füße selbst. Immer schlug er zu, flog dann unruhig mehrmals um mich und setzte dann die Arbeit fort. Es kam ein Herr vorüber, sah ein Weilchen zu und fragte dann, warum ich den Geier dulde. »Ich bin ja wehrlos,« sagte ich, »er kam und fing zu hacken an, da wollte ich ihn natürlich wegtreiben, versuchte ihn sogar zu würgen, aber ein solches Tier hat große Kräfte, auch wollte er mir schon ins Gesicht springen, da opferte ich lieber die Füße. Nun sind sie schon fast zerrissen.« »Daß Sie sich so quälen lassen,« sagte der Herr, »ein Schuß und der Geier ist erledigt.« »Ist das so?« fragte ich, »und wollen Sie das besorgen?« »Gern,« sagte der Herr, »ich muß nur nach Hause gehn und mein Gewehr holen. Können Sie noch eine halbe Stunde warten?« »Das weiß ich nicht,« sagte ich und stand eine Weile starr vor Schmerz, dann sagte ich: »Bitte, versuchen Sie es für jeden Fall.« »Gut,« sagte der Herr, »ich werde mich beeilen.« Der Geier hatte während des Gespräches ruhig zugehört und die Blicke zwischen mir und dem Herrn wandern lassen. Jetzt sah ich, daß er alles verstanden hatte, er flog auf, weit beugte er sich zurück, um genug Schwung zu bekommen und stieß dann wie ein Speerwerfer den Schnabel durch meinen Mund tief in mich. Zurückfallend fühlte ich befreit, wie er in meinem alle Tiefen füllenden, alle Ufer überfließendem Blut unrettbar ertrank.

148

A vulture was hacking at my feet. It had already torn my boots and stockings to shreds, now it was hacking at the feet themselves. Again and again it struck at them, then circled several times restlessly round me, then returned to continue its work. A gentleman passed by, looked on for a while, then asked me why I suffered the vulture. "I'm helpless," I said. "When it came and began to attack me, I of course tried to drive it away, even to strangle it, but these animals are very strong, it was about to spring at my face, but I preferred to sacrifice my feet. Now they are almost torn to bits." "Fancy letting yourself be tortured like this!" said the gentleman. "One shot and that's the end of the vulture." "Really?" I said. "And would you do that?" "With pleasure," said the gentleman, "I've only got to go home and get my gun. Could you wait another half hour?" "I'm not sure about that," said I, and stood for a moment rigid with pain. Then I said: "Do try it in any case, please." "Very well," said the gentleman, "I'll be as quick as I can." During this conversation the vulture had been calmly listening, letting its eye rove between me and the gentleman. Now I realized that it had understood everything; it took wing, leaned far back to gain impetus, and then, like a javelin thrower, thrust its beak through my mouth, deep into me. Falling back, I was relieved to feel him drowning irretrievably in my blood, which was filling every depth, flooding every shore.

Es öffnete sich die Tür und es kam, gut im Saft, an den Seiten üppig gerundet, fußlos mit der ganzen Unterseite sich vorschiebend, der grüne Drache ins Zimmer herein. Formelle Begrüßung. Ich bat ihn, völlig einzutreten. Er bedauerte dies nicht tun zu können, da er zu lang sei. Die Tür mußte also offen bleiben, was recht peinlich war. Er lächelte halb verlegen, halb tückisch und begann: »Durch deine Sehnsucht herangezogen, schiebe ich mich von weither heran, bin unten schon ganz wundgescheuert. Aber ich tue es gerne. Gerne komme ich, gerne biete ich mich dir an.«

The door opened and what entered the room, fat
and succulent, its sides voluptuously swelling, footless,
pushing itself along on its entire underside, was the
green dragon. Formal salutation. I asked him to come
right in. He regretted that he could not do that, as
he was too long. This meant that the door had to remain open, which was rather awkward. He smiled,
half in embarrassment, half cunningly, and began:

"Drawn hither by your longing, I come pushing myself along from afar off, and underneath am now
scraped quite sore. But I am glad to do it. Gladly do
I come, gladly do I offer myself to you."

Dem berühmten Dresseur Burson wurde einmal ein Tiger vorgeführt; er sollte sich über die Dressurfähigkeit des Tieres äußern. In den Dressurkäfig, der die Ausmaße eines Saals hatte—er stand in einem großen Barackenhain weit vor der Stadt—wurde der kleine Käfig mit dem Tiger geschoben. Die Wärter entfernten sich, Burson wollte bei jeder ersten Begegnung mit einem Tier völlig allein sein. Der Tiger lag still, er war eben reichlich gefüttert worden. Ein wenig gähnte er, sah müde die neue Umgebung an und schlief gleich ein.

Once a tiger was brought to the celebrated animal tamer Burson, for him to give his opinion as to the possibility of taming the animal. The small cage with the tiger in it was pushed into the training cage, which had the dimensions of a public hall; it was in a large hut-camp a long way outside the town. The attendants withdrew: Burson always wanted to be completely alone with an animal at his first encounter with it. The tiger lay quiet, having just been plentifully fed. It yawned a little, gazed wearily at its new surroundings, and immediately fell asleep.

Unsere Gesetze sind nicht allgemein bekannt, sie sind Geheimnis der kleinen Adelsgruppe, welche uns beherrscht. Wir sind davon überzeugt, dass diese alten Gesetze genau eingehalten werden, aber es ist doch etwas äusserst Quälendes, nach Gesetzen beherrscht zu werden, die man nicht kennt. Ich denke hierbei nicht an die verschiedenen Auslegungsmöglichkeiten und die Nachteile, die es mit sich bringt, wenn nur einzelne und nicht das ganze Volk an der Auslegung sich beteiligen dürfen. Diese Nachteile sind vielleicht gar nicht sehr gross. Die Gesetze sind ja so alt, Jahrhunderte haben an ihrer Auslegung gearbeitet, auch diese Auslegung ist wohl schon Gesetz geworden, die möglichen Freiheiten bei der Auslegung bestehen zwar immer noch, sind aber sehr eingeschränkt. Ausserdem hat offenbar der Adel keinen Grund, sich bei der Auslegung von seinem persönlichen Interesse zu unseren Ungunsten beeinflussen zu lassen, denn die Gesetze sind ja von ihrem Beginne an für den Adel festgelegt worden, der Adel steht ausserhalb des Gesetzes, und gerade deshalb scheint das Gesetz sich ausschliesslich in die Hände des Adels gegeben zu haben. Darin liegt natürlich Weisheit—wer zweifelt die Weisheit der alten Gesetze an?—, aber eben auch Qual für uns, wahrscheinlich ist das unumgänglich.

Übrigens können auch diese Scheingesetze eigentlich nur vermutet werden. Es ist eine Tradition, dass sie bestehen und dem Adel als Geheimnis anvertraut sind,

Our laws are not generally known; they are kept secret by the small group of nobles who rule us. We are convinced that these ancient laws are scrupulously administered; nevertheless, it is an extremely painful thing to be ruled by laws that one does not know. I am not thinking of possible discrepancies that may arise in the interpretation of the laws, or of the disadvantages involved when only a few and not the whole people are allowed to have a say in their interpretation. These disadvantages are perhaps of no great importance. For the laws are very ancient; their interpretation has been the work of centuries, and has itself doubtless acquired the status of law; and though there is still a possible freedom of interpretation left, it has now become very restricted. Moreover the nobles have obviously no cause to be influenced in their interpretation by personal interests inimical to us, for the laws were made to the advantage of the nobles from the very beginning, they themselves stand above the laws, and that seems to be why the laws were entrusted exclusively into their hands. Of course, there is wisdom in that—who doubts the wisdom of the ancient laws?—but also hardship for us; probably that is unavoidable.

The very existence of these laws, however, is at most a matter of presumption. There is a tradition that they exist and that they are a mystery confided to the nobility, but it is not and cannot be more than a mere tradition sanctioned by age, for the essence of a secret code

aber mehr als alte und durch ihr Alter glaubwürdige
Tradition ist es nicht und kann es nicht sein, denn der
Charakter dieser Gesetze verlangt auch das Geheim-
halten ihres Bestandes. Wenn wir im Volk aber seit
ältesten Zeiten die Handlungen des Adels aufmerksam
verfolgen, Aufschreibungen unserer Voreltern darüber
besitzen, sie gewissenhaft fortgesetzt haben und in den
zahllosen Tatsachen gewisse Richtlinien zu erkennen
glauben, die auf diese oder jene geschichtliche Bestimmung schliessen lassen, und wenn wir nach diesen
sorgfältigst gesiebten und geordneten Schlussfolge-
rungen uns für die Gegenwart und Zukunft ein wenig
einzurichten suchen—so ist das alles unsicher und
vielleicht nur ein Spiel des Verstandes, denn vielleicht bestehen diese Gesetze, die wir hier zu erraten
suchen, überhaupt nicht. Es gibt eine kleine Partei,
die wirklich dieser Meinung ist und die nach-
zuweisen versucht, dass, wenn ein Gesetz besteht,
es nur lauten kann: Was der Adel tut, ist Gesetz. Diese
Partei sieht nur Willkürakte des Adels und verwirft
die Volkstradition, die ihrer Meinung nach nur
geringen zufälligen Nutzen bringt, dagegen meistens
schweren Schaden, da sie dem Volk den kommenden
Ereignissen gegenüber eine falsche, trügerische, zu
Leichtsinn führende Sicherheit gibt. Dieser Schaden
ist nicht zu leugnen, aber die bei weitem überwiegende
Mehrheit unseres Volkes sieht die Ursache dessen
darin, dass die Tradition noch bei weitem nicht aus-
reicht, dass also noch viel mehr in ihr geforscht
werden muss, und dass allerdings auch ihr Material, so
riesenhaft es scheint, noch viel zu klein ist, und dass

is that it should remain a mystery. Some of us among the people have attentively scrutinized the doings of the nobility since the earliest times and possess records made by our forefathers—records which we have conscientiously continued—and claim to recognize amid the countless number of facts certain main tendencies which permit of this or that historical formulation; but when in accordance with these scrupulously tested and logically ordered conclusions we seek to orient ourselves somewhat towards the present or the future, everything becomes uncertain, and our work seems only an intellectual game, for perhaps these laws that we are trying to unravel do not exist at all. There is a small party who are actually of this opinion and who try to show that, if any law exists, it can only be this: The Law is whatever the nobles do. This party see everywhere only the arbitrary acts of the nobility, and reject the popular tradition, which according to them possesses only certain trifling and incidental advantages that do not offset its heavy drawbacks, for it gives the people a false, deceptive and over-confident security in confronting coming events. This cannot be gainsaid, but the overwhelming majority of our people account for it by the fact that the tradition is far from complete and must be more fully enquired into, that the material available, prodigious as it looks, is still too meager, and that several centuries will have to pass before it becomes really adequate. This view, so comfortless as far as the present is concerned, is lightened only by the belief that a time will eventually come when the tradition and our research into it will jointly reach their conclusion, and

noch Jahrhunderte vergehen müssen, ehe es genügen wird. Das für die Gegenwart Trübe dieses Ausblicks erhellt nur der Glaube, dass einmal eine Zeit kommen wird, wo die Tradition und ihre Forschung gewissermassen aufatmend den Schlusspunkt macht, alles klar geworden ist, das Gesetz nur dem Volk gehört, und der Adel verschwindet. Das wird nicht etwa mit Hass gegen den Adel gesagt, durchaus nicht und von niemandem. Eher hassen wir uns selbst, weil wir noch nicht des Gesetzes gewürdigt werden können. Und darum eigentlich ist jene in gewissem Sinn doch sehr verlockende Partei, welche an kein eigentliches Gesetz glaubt, so klein geblieben, weil auch sie den Adel und das Recht seines Bestandes vollkommen anerkennt.

Man kann es eigentlich nur in einer Art Widerspruch ausdrücken: Eine Partei, die neben dem Glauben an die Gesetze auch den Adel verwerfen würde, hätte sofort das ganze Volk hinter sich, aber eine solche Partei kann nicht entstehen, weil den Adel niemand zu verwerfen wagt. Auf dieses Messers Schneide leben wir. Ein Schriftsteller hat das einmal so zusammengefasst: Das einzige, sichtbare, zweifellose Gesetz, das uns auferlegt ist, ist der Adel, und um dieses einzige Gesetz sollten wir uns selbst bringen wollen?

as it were gain a breathing space, when everything will have become clear, the law will belong to the people, and the nobility will vanish. This is not maintained in any spirit of hatred against the nobility; not at all, and by no one. We are more inclined to hate ourselves, because we have not yet shown ourselves worthy of being entrusted with the laws. And that is the real reason why the party which believes that there is no law has remained so small—although its doctrine is in certain ways so attractive, for it unequivocally recognizes the nobility and its right to go on existing.

Actually one can express the problem only in a sort of paradox: Any party which would repudiate, not only all belief in the laws, but the nobility as well, would have the whole people behind it; yet no such party can come into existence, for nobody would dare to repudiate the nobility. We live on this razor edge. A writer once summed the matter up in this way: The sole visible and indubitable law that is imposed upon us is the nobility, and must we ourselves deprive ourselves of that one law?

Unser Städtchen liegt nicht etwa an der Grenze, bei weitem nicht, zur Grenze ist es noch so weit, daß vielleicht noch niemand aus dem Städtchen dort gewesen ist, wüste Hochländer sind zu durchqueren, aber auch weite fruchtbare Länder. Man wird müde, wenn man sich nur einen Teil des Weges vorstellt, und mehr als einen Teil kann man sich gar nicht vorstellen. Auch große Städte liegen auf dem Weg, viel größer als unser Städtchen. Zehn solche Städtchen, nebeneinander gelegt, und von oben noch zehn solche Städtchen hineingezwängt, ergeben noch keine dieser riesigen und engen Städte. Verirrt man sich nicht auf dem Weg dorthin, so verirrt man sich in den Städten gewiß, und ihnen auszuweichen ist wegen ihrer Größe unmöglich.

Aber doch noch weiter als bis zur Grenze ist, wenn man solche Entfernungen überhaupt vergleichen kann —es ist so, als wenn man sagte, ein dreihundertjähriger Mann ist älter als ein zweihundertjähriger-, also noch viel weiter als bis zur Grenze ist es von unserem Städtchen zur Hauptstadt. Während wir von den Grenzkriegen hie und da doch Nachrichten bekommen, erfahren wir aus der Hauptstadt fast nichts, wir bürgerlichen Leute meine ich, denn die Regierungsbeamten haben allerdings eine sehr gute Verbindung mit der Hauptstadt, in zwei, drei Monaten können sie schon eine Nachricht von dort haben, wenigstens behaupten sie es.

Our little town does not lie on the frontier, nowhere near; it is so far from the frontier, in fact, that perhaps no one from our town has ever been there; desolate highlands have to be crossed as well as wide fertile plains. To imagine even part of the road makes one tired, and more than part one just cannot imagine. There are also big towns on the road, each far larger than ours. Ten little towns like ours laid side by side, and ten more forced down from above, still would not produce one of these enormous, overcrowded towns. If one does not get lost on the way one is bound to lose oneself in these towns, and to avoid them is impossible on account of their size.

But what is even further from our town than the frontier, if such distances can be compared at all—it's like saying that a man of three hunderd years is older than one of two hundred—what is even further than the frontier is the capital. Whereas we do get news of the frontier wars now and again, of the capital we learn next to nothing—we civilians that is, for of course the government officials have very good connections with the capital; they can get news from there in as little as three months, so they claim at least.

Now it is remarkable and I am continually being surprised at the way we in our town humbly submit to all orders issued in the capital. For centuries no political change has been brought about by the citizens

Und nun ist es merkwürdig, und darüber wundere ich mich immer wieder von neuem, wie wir uns in unserem Städtchen allem ruhig fügen, was von der Hauptstadt aus angeordnet wird. Seit Jahrhunderten hat bei uns keine, von den Bürgern selbst ausgehende politische Veränderung stattgefunden. In der Hauptstadt haben die hohen Herrscher einander abgelöst, ja sogar Dynastien sind ausgelöscht oder abgesetzt worden und neue haben begonnen, im vorigen Jahrhundert ist sogar die Hauptstadt selbst zerstört, eine neue weit von ihr gegründet, später auch diese zerstört und die alter wieder aufgebaut worden, auf unser Städtchen hat das eigentlich keinen Einfluß gehabt. Unsere Beamtenschaft war immer auf ihrem Posten, die höchsten Beamten kamen aus der Hauptstadt, die mittleren Beamten zumindest von auswärts, die niedrigsten aus unserer Mitte, und so blieb es und so hat es uns genügt. Der höchste Beamte ist der Obersteuereinnehmer, er hat den Rang eines Obersten und wird auch so genannt. Heute ist er ein alter Mann, ich kenne ihn aber schon seit Jahren, denn schon in meiner Kindheit war er Oberst, er hat zuerst eine sehr schnelle Karriere gemacht, dann scheint sie aber gestockt zu haben, nun für unser Städtchen reicht sein Rang aus, einen höheren Rang wären wir bei uns gar nicht aufzunehmen fähig. Wann ich mir ihn vorzustellen suche, sehe ich ihn auf der Veranda seines Hauses auf dem Marktplatz sitzen, zurückgelehnt, die Pfeife im Mund. Über ihm weht vom Dach die Reichsfahne, an den Seiten der Veranda, die so groß ist, daß dort manchmal auch kleine militärische Übungen

themselves. In the capital great rulers have superseded each other—indeed, even dynasties have been deposed or annihilated, and new ones have started; in the past century even the capital itself was destroyed, a new one was founded far away from it, later on this too was destroyed and the old one rebuilt, yet none of this had any influence on our little town. Our officials have always remained at their posts; the highest officials came from the capital, the less high from other towns, and the lowest from among ourselves—that is how is has always been and it has suited us. The highest official is the chief tax-collector, he has the rank of colonel, and is known as such. The present one is an old man; I've known him for years, because he was already a colonel when I was a child. At first he rose very fast in his career, but then he seems to have advanced no further; actually, for our little town his rank is good enough, a higher rank would be out of place. When I try to recall him I see him sitting on the veranda of his house in the Market Square, leaning back, pipe in mouth. Above him from the roof flutters the imperial flag; on the sides of the veranda, which is so big that minor military maneuvers are sometimes held there, washing hangs out to dry. His grandchildren, in beautiful silk clothes, play around him; they are not allowed down in the Market Square, the children there are considered unworthy of them, but the grandchildren are attracted by the Square, so they thrust their heads between the posts of the banister and when the children below begin to quarrel they join the quarrel from above.

stattfinden, ist die Wäsche zum Trocknen aufgehängt. Seine Enkel, in schönen seidenen Kleidern, spielen um ihn herum, auf den Marktplatz hinunter dürfen sie nicht gehn, die andern Kinder sind ihrer unwürdig, aber doch lockt sie der Platz und sie stecken wenigstens die Köpfe zwischen den Geländerstangen durch und wenn die andern Kinder unten streiten, streiten sie von oben mit.

Dieser Oberst also beherrscht die Stadt. Ich glaube, er hat noch niemandem ein Dokument vorgezeigt, das ihn dazu berechtigt. Er hat wohl auch kein solches Dokument. Vielleicht ist er wirklich Obersteuereinnehmer. Aber ist das alles? Berechtigt ihn das, auch in allen Gebieten der Verwaltung zu herrschen? Sein Amt ist ja für den Staat sehr gewichtig, aber für die Bürger ist es doch nicht das Wichtigste. Bei uns hat man fast den Eindruck, als ob die Leute sagten: »Nun hast du uns alles genommen, was wir hatten, nimm bitte auch uns selbst noch dazu. «Denn tatsächlich hat er nicht etwa die Herrschaft an sich gerissen und ist auch kein Tyrann. Es hat sich seit alten Zeiten so entwickelt, daß der Obersteuereinnehmer der erste Beamte ist, und der Oberst fügt sich dieser Tradition nicht anders als wir.

Aber wiewohl er ohne allzuviel Unterscheidungen der Würde unter uns lebt, ist er doch etwas ganz anderes als die gewöhnlichen Bürger. Wenn eine Abordnung mit einer Bitte vor ihn kommt, steht er da wie die Mauer der Welt. Hinter ihm ist nichts mehr, man hört förmlich dort weiterhin noch ahnungsweise ein paar Stimmen flüstern, aber das ist wahrscheinlich Täuschung, er bedeutet doch den Abschluß des Ganzen,

This colonel, then, commands the town. I don't think he has ever produced a document entitling him to this position; very likely he does not possess such a thing. Maybe he really is chief tax-collector. But is that all? Does that entitle him to rule over all the other departments in the administration as well? True, his office is very important for the government, but for the citizens it is hardly the most important. One is almost under the impression that the people here say: "Now that you've taken all we possess, please take us as well." In reality, of course, it was not he who seized the power, nor is he a tyrant. It has just come about over the years that the chief tax-collector is automatically the top official, and the colonel accepts the tradition just as we do.

Yet while he lives among us without laying too much stress on his official position, he is something quite different from the ordinary citizen. When a delegation comes to him with a request, he stands there like the wall of the world. Behind him is nothingness, one imagines hearing voices whispering in the background, but this is probably a delusion; after all, he represents the end of all things, at least for us. At these receptions he really was worth seeing. Once as a child I was present when a delegation of citizens arrived to ask him for a government subsidy because the poorest quarter of the town had been burned to the ground. My father the blacksmith, a man well respected in the community, was a member of the delegation and had taken me along. There's nothing exceptional about this, everyone rushes to spectacles of this kind, one can hardly distinguish the actual dele-

wenigstens für uns. Man muß ihn bei solchen Empfängen gesehen haben. Als Kind war ich einmal dabei, als eine Abordnung der Bürgerschaft ihn um eine Regierungsunterstützung bat, denn das ärmste Stadtviertel war gänzlich niedergebrannt. Mein Vater, der Hufschmied, ist in der Gemeinde angesehen, war Mitglied der Abordnung und hatte mich mitgenommen. Das ist nichts Außergewöhnliches, zu einem solchen Schauspiel drängt sich alles, man erkennt die eigentliche Abordnung kaum aus der Menge heraus; da solche Empfänge meist auf der Verande stattfinden, gibt es auch Leute, die vom Marktplatz her auf Leitern hinaufklettern und über das Geländer hinweg an den Dingen oben teilnehmen. Damals war es so eingerichtet, daß etwa ein Viertel der Veranda ihm vorbehalten war, den übrigen Teil füllte die Menge. Einige Soldaten überwachten alles, auch umstanden sie in einem Halbkreis ihn selbst. Im Grunde hätte ein Soldat für alles genügt, so groß ist bei uns die Furcht vor ihnen. Ich weiß nicht genau, woher diese Soldaten kommen, jedenfalls von weit her, alle sind sie einander sehr ähnlich, sie würden nicht einmal eine Uniform brauchen. Es sind kleine, nicht starke, aber behende Leute, am auffallendsten ist an ihnen das starke Gebiß, das förmlich allzusehr ihren Mund füllt, und ein gewisses unruhig zuckendes Blitzen ihrer kleinen schmalen Augen. Durch dieses sind sie der Schrecken der Kinder, allerdings auch ihre Lust, denn immerfort möchten die Kinder vor diesem Gebiß und diesen Augen erschrecken wollen, um dann verzweifelt wegzulaufen. Dieser Schrecken aus der Kinderzeit verliert

gation from the crowd. Since these receptions usually take place on the veranda, there are even people who climb up by ladder from the Market Square and take part in the goings-on from over the banister. On this occasion about a quarter of the veranda had been reserved for the colonel, the crowd filling the rest of it. A few soldiers kept watch, some of them standing round him in a semicircle. Actually a single soldier would have been quite enough, such is our fear of them. I don't know exactly where these soldiers come from, in any case from a long way off, they all look very much alike, they wouldn't even need a uniform. They are small, not strong but agile people, the most striking thing about them is the prominence of their teeth which almost overcrowd their mouths, and a certain restless twitching of their small narrow eyes. This makes them the terror of the children, but also their delight, for again and again the children long to be frightened by these teeth, these eyes, so as to be able to run away in horror. Even grownups probably never quite lose this childish terror, at least it continues to have an effect. There are, of course, other factors contributing to it. The soldiers speak a dialect utterly incomprehensible to us, and they can hardly get used to ours—all of which produces a certain shut-off, unapproachable quality corresponding, as it happens, to their character, for they are silent, serious, and rigid. They don't actually do anything evil, and yet they are almost unbearable in an evil sense. A soldier, for example, enters a shop, buys some trifling object, and stays there leaning against the counter; he

sich wahrscheinlich auch bei den Erwachsenen nicht, zumindest wirkt er nach. Es kommt dann freilich auch noch anderes hinzu. Die Soldaten sprechen einen uns ganz unverständlichen Dialekt, können sich an unsern kaum gewöhnen, dadurch ergibt sich bei ihnen eine gewisse Abgeschlossenheit, Unnahbarkeit, die überdies auch ihrem Charakter entspricht, so still, ernst und starr sind sie, sie tun nichts eigentlich Böses und sind doch in einem bösen Sinn fast unerträglich. Es kommt zum Beispiel ein Soldat in ein Geschäft, kauft eine Kleinigkeit, und bleibt dort nun an den Pult gelehnt stehn, hört den Gesprächen zu, versteht sie wahrscheinlich nicht, aber es hat doch den Anschein, als ob er sie verstünde, sagt selbst kein Wort, blickt nur starr auf den, welcher spricht, dann wieder auf die, welche zuhören, und hält die Hand auf dem Griff des langen Messers in seinem Gürtel. Das ist abscheulich, man verliert die Lust an der Unterhaltung, der Laden leert sich, und erst wenn er ganz leer ist, geht auch der Soldat. Wo also die Soldaten auftreten, wird auch unser lebhaftes Volk still. So war es auch damals. Wie bei allen feierlichen Gelegenheiten stand der Oberst aufrecht und hielt mit den nach vorn ausgestreckten Händen zwei lange Bambusstangen. Es ist eine alte Sitte, die etwa bedeutet: so stützt er das Gesetz und so stützt es ihn. Nun weiß ja jeder, was ihn oben auf der Veranda erwartet, und doch pflegt man immer wieder von neuem zu erschrecken, auch damals wollte der zum Reden Bestimmte nicht anfangen, er stand schon dem Obersten gegenüber, aber dann verließ ihn der Mut und er drängte sich wieder

listens to the conversations, probably does not understand them, and yet gives the impression of understanding; he himself does not say a word, just stares blankly at the speaker, then back at the listeners, all the while keeping his hand on the hilt of the long knife in his belt. This is revolting, one loses the desire to talk, the customers start leaving the shop, and only when it is quite empty does the soldier also leave. Thus wherever the soldiers appear, our lively people grow silent. That's what happened this time, too. As on all solemn occasions the colonel stood upright, holding in front of him two poles of bamboo in his outstretched hands. This is an ancient custom implying more or less that he supports the law, and the law supports him. Now everyone knows, of course, what to expect up on the veranda, and yet each time people take fright all over again. On this occasion, too, the man chosen to speak could not begin; he was already standing opposite the colonel when his courage failed him and, muttering a few excuses, he pushed his way back into the crowd. No other suitable person willing to speak could be found, albeit several unsuitable ones offered themselves; a great commotion ensued and messengers were sent in search of various citizens who were well-known speakers. During all this time the colonel stood there motionless, only his chest moving visibly up and down to his breathing. Not that he breathed with difficulty, it was just that he breathed so conspicuously, much as frogs breathe—except that with them it is normal, while here it was exceptional. I squeezed myself through the grownups and watched

unter verschiedenen Ausreden in die Menge zurück.
Auch sonst fand sich kein Geeigneter, der bereit gewesen wäre zu sprechen—von den Ungeeigneten boten sich allerdings einige an , es war eine große Verwirrung und man sandte Boten an verschiedene Bürger, bekannte Redner aus. Während dieser ganzen
Zeit stand der Oberst unbeweglich da, nur im Atmen
senkte sich auffallend die Brust. Nicht daß er etwa
schwer geatmet hätte, er atmete nur äußerst deutlich,
so wie zum Beispiel Frösche atmen, nur daß es bei
ihnen immer so ist, hier aber war es außerordentlich.
Ich schlich mich zwischen den Erwachsenen durch
und beobachtete ihn durch die Lücke zwischen zwei
Soldaten so lange, bis mich einer mit dem Knie weg-
stieß. Inzwischen hatte sich der ursprünglich zum
Redner Bestimmte gesammelt und, von zwei Mit-
bürgern fest gestützt, hielt er die Ansprache. Rührend
war, wie er bei dieser ernsten, das große Unglück
schildernden Rede immer lächelte, ein allerde-
mütigstes Lächeln, das sich vergeblich anstrengte auch
nur einen leichten Widerschein auf dem Gesicht des
Obersten hervorzurufen. Schließlich formulierte er
die Bitte, ich glaube, er bat nur um Steuerbefreiung
für ein Jahr, vielleicht aber auch noch um bil-
ligeres Bauholz aus den kaiserlichen Wäldern. Dann
verbeugte er sich tief und blieb in der Verbeugung,
ebenso wie alle andern außer dem Obersten, den
Soldaten und einigen Beamten im Hintergrund. Lä-
cherlich war es für das Kind, wie die auf den Leitern
am Verandarand ein paar Sprossen hinunterstiegen,
um während dieser entscheidenden Pause nicht ge-

him through a gap between two soldiers, until one of them kicked me away with his knee. Meanwhile the man originally chosen to speak had regained his composure and, firmly held up by two fellow citizens, was delivering his address. It was touching to see him smile throughout this solemn speech describing a grievous misfortune—a most humble smile which strove in vain to elicit some slight reaction on the colonel's face. Finally he formulated the request—I think he was only asking for a year's tax exemption, but possibly also for timber from the imperial forests at a reduced price. Then he bowed low, remaining in this position for some time, as did everyone else except the colonel, the soldiers, and a number of officials in the background. To the child it seemed ridiculous that the people on the ladders should climb down a few rungs so as not to be seen during the significant pause and now and again peer inquisitively over the floor of the veranda. After this had lasted quite a while an official, a little man, stepped up to the colonel and tried to reach the latter's height by standing on his toes. The colonel, still motionless save for his deep breathing, whispered something in his ear, whereupon the little man clapped his hands and everyone rose. "The petition has been refused," he announced. "You may go." An undeniable sense of relief passed through the crowd, everyone surged out, hardly a soul paying any special attention to the colonel, who, as it were, had turned once more into a human being like the rest of us. I still caught one last glimpse of him as he wearily let go of the poles,

sehen zu werden, und nur neugierig unten knapp über dem Boden der Veranda von Zeit zu Zeit spionierten. Das dauerte eine Weile, dann trat ein Beamter, ein kleiner Mann, vor den Obersten, suchte sich auf den Fußspitzen zu ihm emporzuheben, erhielt von ihm, der noch immer bis auf das tiefe Atmen unbeweglich blieb, etwas ins Ohr geflüstert, klatschte in die Hände, worauf sich alle erhoben, und verkündete: »Die Bitte ist abgewiesen. Entfernt euch.« Ein unleugbares Gefühl der Erleichterung ging durch die Menge, alles drängte sich hinaus, auf den Obersten, der förmlich wieder ein Mensch wie wir alle geworden war, achtete kaum jemand besonders, ich sah nur, wie er tatsächlich erschöpft die Stangen losließ, die hinfielen, in einen von Beamten herbeigeschleppten Lehnstuhl sank und eilig die Tabakpfeife in den Mund schob.

Dieser ganze Vorfall ist nicht vereinzelt, so geht es allgemein zu. Es kommt zwar vor, daß hie und da kleine Bitten erfüllt werden, aber dann ist es so, als hätte das der Oberst auf eigene Verantwortung als mächtige Privatperson getan, es muß—gewiß nicht ausdrücklich, aber der Stimmung nach—förmlich vor der Regierung geheimgehalten werden. Nun sind ja in unserem Städtchen die Augen des Obersten, soweit wir es beurteilen können, auch die Augen der Regierung, aber doch wird hier ein Unterschied gemacht, in den vollständig nicht einzudringen ist.

In wichtigen Angelegenheiten aber kann die Bürgerschaft einer Abweisung immer sicher sein. Und nun ist es eben so merkwürdig, daß man ohne diese Abweisung gewissermaßen nicht auskommen kann und

which fell to the ground, then sank into an armchair produced by some officials, and promptly put his pipe in his mouth.

This whole occurrence is not isolated, it's in the general run of things. Indeed, it does happen now and again that minor petitions are granted, but then it invariably looks as though the colonel had done it as a powerful private person on his own responsibility, and it had to be kept all but a secret from the government—not explicitly of course, but that is what it feels like. No doubt in our little town the colonel's eyes, so far as we know, are also the eyes of the government, and yet there is a difference which it is impossible to comprehend completely.

In all important matters, however, the citizens can always count on a refusal. And now the strange fact is that without this refusal one simply cannot get along, yet at the same time these official occasions designed to receive the refusal are by no means a formality. Time after time one goes there full of expectation and in all seriousness and then one returns, if not exactly strengthened or happy, nevertheless not disappointed or tired. About these things I do not have to ask the opinion of anyone else, I feel them in myself, as everyone does; nor do I have any great desire to find out how these things are connected.

As a matter of fact there is, so far as my observations go, a certain age group that is not content—these are the young people roughly between seventeen and twenty. Quite young fellows, in fact, who are utterly

dabei ist dieses Hingehn und Abholen der Abweisung durchaus keine Formalität. Immer wieder frisch und ernst geht man hin und geht dann wieder von dort, allerdings nicht geradezu gekräftigt und beglückt, aber doch auch gar nicht enttäuscht und müde. Ich muß mich bei niemandem nach diesen Dingen erkundigen, ich fühle es in mir selbst wie alle. Und nicht einmal eine gewisse Neugierde, den Zusammenhängen dieser Dinge nachzuforschen.

Es gibt allerdings, so weit meine Beobachtungen reichen, eine gewisse Altersklasse, die nicht zufrieden ist, es sind etwa die jungen Leute zwischen siebzehn und zwanzig. Also ganz junge Burschen, die die Tragweite des unbedeutendsten, wie erst gar eines revolutionären Gedankens nicht von der Ferne ahnen können. Und gerade unter sie schleicht sich die Unzufriedenheit ein.

KURIERE

Es wurde ihnen die Wahl gestellt, Könige oder der Könige Kuriere zu werden. Nach Art der Kinder wollten alle Kuriere sein. Deshalb gibt es lauter Kuriere, sie jagen durch die Welt und rufen, da es keine Könige gibt, einander selbst die sinnlos gewordenen Meldungen zu. Gerne würden sie ihrem elenden Leben ein Ende machen, aber sie wagen es nicht wegen des Diensteides.

174

incapable of foreseeing the consequences of even the least significant, far less a revolutionary, idea. And it is among just them that discontent creeps in.

COURIERS

They were offered the choice between becoming kings or the couriers of kings. The way children would, they all wanted to be couriers. Therefore there are only couriers who hurry about the world, shouting to each other—since there are no kings—messages that have become meaningless. They would like to put an end to this miserable life of theirs but they dare not because of their oaths of service.

Es war einmal ein Geduldspiel, ein billiges einfaches Spiel, nicht viel größer als eine Taschenuhr und ohne irgendwelche überraschende Einrichtungen. In der rotbraun angestrichenen Holzfläche waren einige blaue Irrwege eingeschnitten, die in eine kleine Grube mündeten. Die gleichfalls blaue Kugel war durch Neigen und Schütteln zunächst in einen der Wege zu bringen und dann in die Grube. War die Kugel in der Grube, dann war das Spiel zu Ende, wollte man es von neuem beginnen, mußte man die Kugel wieder aus der Grube schütteln. Bedeckt war das Ganze von einem starken gewölbten Glas, man konnte das Geduldspiel in die Tasche stecken und mitnehmen und wo immer man war, konnte man es hervornehmen und spielen.

War die Kugel unbeschäftigt, so ging sie meistens, die Hände auf dem Rücken, auf der Hochebene hin und her, die Wege vermied sie. Sie war der Ansicht, daß sie während des Spieles genug mit den Wegen gequält werde und daß sie reichlichen Anspruch darauf habe, wenn nicht gespielt würde, sich auf der freien Ebene zu erholen. Manchmal sah sie gewohnheitsmäßig zu dem gewölbten Glase auf, doch ohne die Absicht, oben etwas zu erkennen. Sie hatte einen breitspurigen Gang und behauptete, daß sie nicht für die schmalen Wege gemacht sei. Das war zum Teil richtig, denn die Wege konnten sie wirklich kaum fassen, es war aber auch unrichtig, denn tatsächlich war sie sehr sorgfältig

Once there was a Chinese puzzle, a cheap simple toy, not much bigger than a pocket watch and without any sort of surprising contrivances. Cut into the flat wood, which was painted reddish-brown, there were some blue labyrinthine paths, which all led into a little hole. The ball, which was also blue, had to be got into one of the paths by means of tilting and shaking the box, and then into the hole. Once the ball was in the hole, the game was over, and if one wanted to start all over again, one had first to shake the ball out of the hole. The whole thing was covered over with a strong, convex glass, one could put the puzzle in one's pocket and carry it about with one, and wherever one was, one could take it out and play with it.

If the ball was unemployed, it spent most of the time strolling to and fro, its hands clasped behind its back, on the plateau, avoiding the paths. It held the view that it was quite enough bothered with the paths during the game and that it had every right to re-cuperate on the open plain when no game was going on. Sometimes it would look up at the vaulted glass, but merely out of habit and quite without any inten-tion of trying to make out anything up there. It had a rather straddling gait and maintained that it was not made for those narrow paths. That was partly true, for indeed the paths could hardly contain it, but it was also untrue, for the fact was that it was very carefully made to fit the width of the paths exactly,

der Breite der Wege angepaßt, bequem aber durften
ihr die Wege nicht sein, denn sonst wäre es kein
Geduldspiel gewesen.

DIE WAHRHEIT ÜBER SANCHO PANSA

Sancho Pansa, der sich übrigens dessen nie gerühmt
hat, gelang es im Laufe der Jahre, durch Beistellung
einer Menge Ritter-und Räuberromane in den Abend-
und Nachtstunden seinen Teufel, dem er später den
Namen Don Quichotte gab, derart von sich abzulenken,
dass dieser dann haltlos die verrücktesten Taten auf-
führte, die aber mangels eines vorbestimmten Gegen-
standes, der eben Sancho Pansa hätte sein sollen,
niemandem schadeten. Sancho Pansa, ein freier Mann,
folgte gleichmütig, vielleicht aus einem gewissen Ver-
antwortlichkeitsgefühl, dem Don Quichotte auf seinen
Zügen und hatte davon eine grosse und nützliche
Unterhaltung bis an sein Ende.

but the paths were certainly not meant to be comfortable for it, or else it would not have been a puzzle at all.

THE TRUTH ABOUT SANCHO PANZA

Without making any boast of it Sancho Panza succeeded in the course of years, by devouring a great number of romances of chivalry and adventure in the evening and night hours, in so diverting from him his demon, whom he later called Don Quixote, that his demon thereupon set out in perfect freedom on the maddest exploits, which, however, for the lack of a preordained object, which should have been Sancho Panza himself, harmed nobody. A free man, Sancho Panza philosophically followed Don Quixote on his crusades, perhaps out of a sense of responsibility, and had of them a great and edifying entertainment to the end of his days.

Ich bin ein Diener, aber es ist keine Arbeit für
mich da. Ich bin ängstlich und dränge mich nicht vor,
ja ich dränge mich nicht einmal in eine Reihe mit
den andern, aber das ist nur die eine Ursache meines
Nichtbeschäftigtseins, es ist auch möglich, daß es mit
meinem Nichtbeschäftigtsein überhaupt nichts zu tun
hat, die Hauptsache ist jedenfalls, daß ich nicht zum
Dienst gerufen werde, andere sind gerufen worden
und haben sich nicht mehr darum beworben als ich, ja
haben vielleicht nicht einmal den Wunsch gehabt,
gerufen zu werden, während ich ihn wenigstens
manchmal sehr stark habe.

So liege ich also auf der Pritsche in der Gesindstube,
schaue zu den Balken auf der Decke hinauf, schlafe
ein, wache auf und schlafe schon wieder ein.
Manchmal gehe ich hinüber ins Wirtshaus, wo ein
saueres Bier ausgeschenkt wird, manchmal habe ich
schon vor Widerwillen ein Glas davon ausgeschüttet,
dann aber trinke ich es wieder. Ich sitze gern dort,
weil ich hinter dem geschlossenen kleinen Fenster,
ohne von irgendjemandem entdeckt werden zu können, zu den Fenstern unseres Hauses hinübersehen
kann. Man sieht ja dort nicht viel, hier gegen die
Straße zu liegen, glaube ich, nur die Fenster der
Korridore und überdies nicht jener Korridore, die zu
den Wohnungen der Herrschaft führen. Es ist möglich, daß ich mich aber auch irre, irgend jemand hat
es einmal, ohne daß ich ihn gefragt hätte, behauptet

I am a servant, but there is no work for me. I am timid and don't push myself to the fore, indeed I don't even push myself into line with the others, but that is only one reason for my nonemployment, it's even possible that it has nothing to do with my nonemployment, in any case the main thing is that I am not called upon to serve, others have been called yet they have not tried harder than I, indeed perhaps they have not even felt the desire to be called, whereas I, at least sometimes, have felt it very strongly.

So I lie on the pallet in the servants' hall, stare at the beams in the ceiling, fall asleep, wake up and promptly fall asleep again. Occasionally I walk over to the tavern where they sell a sour beer, occasionally I have even poured away a glass in disgust, but at other times I drink it. I like sitting there because from behind the closed little window, without the possibility of being discovered, I can see across to the windows of our house. Not that one sees very much there, to my knowledge only the windows of the corridors look out on the street, and moreover not even those of the corridors leading to my employers' apartments. But it is also possible that I am mistaken; someone, without my having asked him, once said so, and the general impression of this house front confirms this. Only rarely are the windows opened, and when this does occur it is done by a servant who may lean against the balustrade to look

und der allgemeine Eindruck dieser Hausfront bestätigt das. Selten nur werden die Fenster geöffnet, und wenn es geschieht, tut es ein Diener und lehnt sich dann wohl auch an die Brüstung, um ein Weilchen hinunterzusehn. Es sind also Korridore, wo er nicht überrascht werden kann. Übrigens kenne ich diese Diener nicht, die ständig oben beschäftigten Diener schlafen anderswo, nicht in meiner Stube.

Einmal, als ich ins Wirtshaus kam, saß auf meinem Beobachtungsplatz schon ein Gast. Ich wagte nicht genau hinzusehn und wollte mich gleich in der Tür wieder umdrehn und weggehn. Aber der Gast rief mich zu sich, und es zeigte sich, daß er auch ein Diener war, den ich schon einmal irgendwo gesehn hatte, ohne aber bisher mit ihm gesprochen zu haben. »Warum willst du fortlaufen? Setz dich her und trink! Ich zahl's.« So setzte ich mich also. Er fragte mich einiges, aber ich konnte es nicht beantworten, ja ich verstand nicht einmal die Fragen. Ich sagte deshalb: »Vielleicht reut es dich jetzt, daß du mich eingeladen hast, dann gehe ich,« und ich wollte schon aufstehn. Aber er langte mit seiner Hand über den Tisch herüber und drückte mich nieder: »Bleib,« sagte er, »das war ja nur eine Prüfung. Wer die Fragen nicht beantwortet, hat die Prüfung bestanden.«

down for a while. It follows therefore that these are corridors where he cannot be taken by surprise. As a matter of fact I am not personally acquainted with these servants; those who are permanently employed upstairs sleep elsewhere, not in my room.

Once when I arrived at the tavern, a guest was sitting at my observation post. I did not dare look at him closely and was about to turn round in the door and leave. The guest, however, called me over, and it turned out that he too was a servant whom I had once seen somewhere before, but without having spoken to him.

"Why do you want to run away? Sit down and have a drink! I'll pay." So I sat down. He asked me several things, but I couldn't answer, indeed I didn't even understand his questions. So I said: "Perhaps you are sorry now that you invited me, so I'd better go," and I was about to get up. But he stretched his hand out over the table and pressed me down. "Stay," he said, "that was only a test. He who does not answer the questions has passed the test."

Hätte Robinson den höchsten oder richtiger den sicht-
barsten Punkt der Insel niemals verlassen, aus Trost
oder Demut oder Furcht oder Unkenntnis oder Sehnsucht, so wäre er bald zugrunde gegangen; da er aber
ohne Rücksicht auf die Schiffe und ihre schwachen
Fernrohre seine ganze Insel zu erforschen und ihrer
sich zu freuen begann, erhielt er sich am Leben und
wurde in einer allerdings dem Verstand notwendigen
Konsequenz schliesslich doch gefunden.

DIE QUELLE

Er hat Durst und ist von der Quelle nur durch ein
Gebüsch getrennt. Er ist aber zweigeteilt, ein Teil
übersieht das Ganze, sieht, daß er hier steht und die
Quelle daneben ist, ein zweiter Teil aber merkt nichts,
hat höchstens eine Ahnung dessen, daß der erste Teil
alles sieht. Da er aber nichts merkt, kann er nicht
trinken.

Had Robinson Crusoe never left the highest, or more correctly the most visible point of his island, from desire for comfort, or timidity, or fear, or ignorance, or longing, he would soon have perished; but since without paying any attention to passing ships and their feeble telescopes he started to explore the whole island and take pleasure in it, he managed to keep himself alive and finally was found after all, by a chain of causality that was, of course, logically inevitable.

THE SPRING

He is thirsty, and is cut off from a spring by a mere clump of bushes. But he is divided against himself: one part overlooks the whole, sees that he is standing here and that the spring is just beside him; but another part notices nothing, has at most a divination that the first part sees all. But as he notices nothing he cannot drink.

Die Unersättlichsten sind manche Asketen, sie machen Hungerstreike auf allen Gebieten des Lebens und wollen dadurch gleichzeitig folgendes erreichen:

1. eine Stimme soll sagen: Genug, du hast genug gefastet, jetzt darfst du essen wie die andern und es wird nicht als Essen angerechnet werden.

2. die gleiche Stimme soll gleichzeitig sagen: Jetzt hast du so lange unter Zwang gefastet, von jetzt an wirst du mit Freude fasten, es wird süßer als Speise sein (gleichzeitig aber wirst du auch wirklich essen),

3. die gleiche Stimme soll gleichzeitig sagen: Du hast die Welt besiegt, ich enthebe dich ihrer, des Essens und des Fastens (gleichzeitig aber wirst du sowohl fasten als essen).

Zudem kommt noch eine seit jeher zu ihnen redende unablässige Stimme: Du fastest zwar nicht vollständig, aber du hast den guten Willen und der genügt.

The most insatiable people are certain ascetics, who go on hunger-strike in all spheres of life, thinking that in this way they will simultaneously achieve the following:

1) a voice will say: Enough, you have fasted enough, now you may eat like the others and it will not be accounted unto you as eating.

2) the same voice will at the same time say: You have fasted for so long under compulsion, from now on you will fast with joy, it will be sweeter than food (at the same time, however, you will also really eat).

3) the same voice will at the same time say: You have conquered the world, I release you from it, as from eating and from fasting (at the same time, however, you will both fast and eat).

In addition to this there also comes a voice that has been speaking to them ceaselessly all the time: Though you do not fast completely, you have the good will, and that suffices.

Ich befahl mein Pferd aus dem Stall zu holen. Der Diener verstand mich nicht. Ich ging selbst in den Stall, sattelte mein Pferd und bestieg es. In der Ferne hörte ich eine Trompete blasen, ich fragte ihn, was das bedeute. Er wußte nichts und hatte nichts gehört. Beim Tore hielt er mich auf und fragte: »Wohin reitest du, Herr?« »Ich weiß es nicht«, sagte ich, »nur weg von hier, nur weg von hier. Immerfort weg von hier, nur so kann ich mein Ziel erreichen.« »Du kennst also dein Ziel?« fragte er. »Ja«, antwortete ich, »ich sagte es doch: ‚Weg-von-hier‘, das ist mein Ziel.« »Du hast keinen Eßvorrat mit«, sagte er. »Ich brauche keinen«, sagte ich, »die Reise ist so lang, daß ich verhungern muß, wenn ich auf dem Weg nichts bekomme. Kein Eßvorrat kann mich retten. Es ist ja zum Glück eine wahrhaft ungeheuere Reise.«

I gave orders for my horse to be brought round from the stable. The servant did not understand me. I myself went to the stable, saddled my horse and mounted. In the distance I heard a bugle call, I asked him what this meant. He knew nothing and had heard nothing. At the gate he stopped me, asking: "Where are you riding to, master?" "I don't know," I said, "only away from here, away from here. Always away from here, only by doing so can I reach my destination." "And so you know your destination?" he asked. "Yes," I answered, "didn't I say so? Away-From-Here, that is my destination." "You have no provisions with you," he said. "I need none," I said, "the journey is so long that I must die of hunger if I don't get anything on the way. No provisions can save me. For it is, fortunately, a truly immense journey."

Epilogue

In the pieces collected in this volume, Frank Kafka re-examined and boldly rewrote some basic mythological tales of Ancient Israel, Hellas, the Far East, and the West, adding to them creations of his own imagination.

The material is drawn from his notebooks and short pieces included in the volumes *Dearest Father, The Great Wall of China, Description of a Struggle;* in his letters, and the novel, *The Trial.*

The original version of this collection appeared under the title *Parables;* for the present edition, additional material has been included.

The following translators have contributed: Clement Greenberg (pp. 21, 41, 47, 81, 85, 93—"The Sirens," 97, 119, 137, 175—"The Couriers"); Ernst Kaiser and Eithne Wilkins (pp. 35—"The Pit," 45, 49, 79, 93—"The Leopards," 95—"Diogenes," 101, 107, 109, 111, 117, 121, 151, 153, 177, 187, 189); Willa and Edwin Muir (pp. 11, 13, 17, 25, 29, 35—"The Tower," 37, 61, 83, 89, 95—"Alexander," 123, 157, 179, 185); and Tania and James Stern (pp. 149, 163, 181). The volume was edited by Nahum N. Glatzer.